BEAR IN THE BACK SEAT

Adventures of a Wildlife Ranger
in the Great Smoky Mountains National Park

BY

Kim DeLozier &
Carolyn Jourdan

Bear in the Back Seat is on
Facebook at www.facebook.com/BlackBearBook
Twitter at twitter.com/BlackBearBook

Cover photo by Bill Lea
www.BillLea.com

Designed by Karen Key

CONTENTS

MAP OF GREAT SMOKY MOUNTAINS

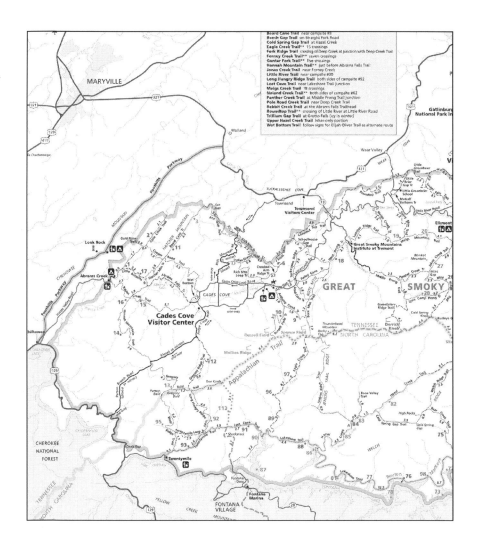

NATIONAL PARK

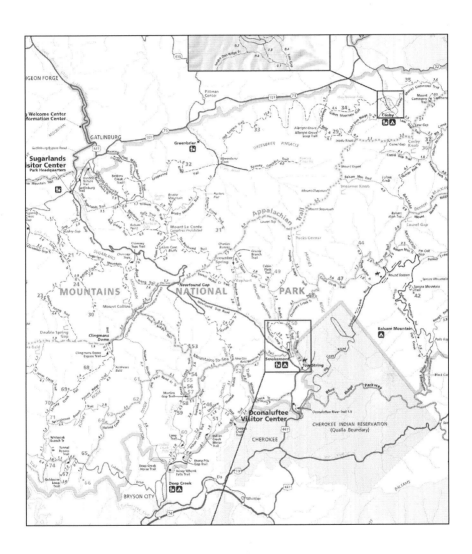

In this book Smoky Mountain dialect is rendered as it sounds. Appalachian speech is poetic and musical. It's sung as much as spoken, so a significant portion of the meaning is conveyed in the cadences and tones.

Dialect is used in conversation by people of all levels of education and intelligence, so no apostrophes will highlight dropped g's or word variants, as if they are errors. For the same reason, the local grammar is retained.

This was done to enable the reader to experience Smoky Mountain life and language intimately, as an insider would.

Wildlife Rangers in the Great Smoky Mountains National Park have developed their own special nomenclature for referring to Park vehicles. These animal nicknames, attributed to Ranger Rick Varner, are based on the size and power of the various trucks.

The Boar: Half-ton 4x4 Dodge pickup with an 8-cylinder engine. It has a winch mounted in the bed to pull cages and traps into the back. This was the most powerful truck. It's the one used to pull the elk trailer or move bear traps that had to be transported in the bed of a truck.

The Sow: Half-ton 4x4 Chevrolet extended cab pickup with a 6-cylinder engine. It has an 8' bed which made the truck difficult to maneuver in tight places. It was good for hauling people when conducting deer counts in Cades Cove. It was big, but not very tough.

The Shoat: Half-ton 4x4 Dodge pickup with a 6-cylinder engine. A medium-strength vehicle used for tasks like towing bear trap trailers or for checking hog traps.

The Piglet: Ford Ranger 4x4 pickup with a small engine. A light-duty vehicle used mainly for checking hog traps and for general transportation.

The Elk Calf: Chevrolet S-10 4x4 pickup with a small engine. A light-duty vehicle used mainly to track and locate elk and for general transportation.

Kim's Truck: Ford Explorer 4x4 SUV with a 6-cylinder engine. It was used for general transportation and elk darting, and occasionally to pull larger trailers for boats. Although this vehicle was sometimes jokingly referred to as the *grocery gitter*, it was Kim's favorite. It earned respect when used to rescue researchers and wildlife handlers after a sudden blizzard in Cataloochee, North Carolina when other vehicles got stuck in the deep snow.

PROLOGUE

WHEN I WAS A KID showing steers in 4-H, I spent a lot of time waiting for someone old enough to drive to come get me and my animal and take us to the fairground. Now, more than thirty years later, I was still waiting for someone to come get me and my animal and take us somewhere. But instead of standing inside a comfortable barn with my hand-raised, immaculately-groomed steer while Dad brought the pickup truck around, this time I was huddled atop a ridge in the Great Smoky Mountains National Park during a fierce windstorm next to a drugged wild black bear, waiting for a stranger to come get us with a helicopter.

The wind was gusting so violently it was hard to imagine how any aircraft could possibly reach us. I prayed they were sending a good pilot. As I waited, I tried to look on the bright side. If I stayed upwind, the naturally pungent smell of the bear wasn't nearly as strong.

I THOUGHT I WANTED to be a full-time farmer. I'd been successful raising and showing cattle and had driven tractors and other farm machinery since I was very young. When I was a senior in high school I'd even won the East Tennessee Future Farmers of America Farm and Skills Tractor Driving Contest. Soon after that I started college, majoring in Agriculture at the University of Tennessee. I began in Animal Science, but several unpleasant incidents with cows on the family farm made me wonder if I shouldn't reconsider my choice.

My first strong hint that farm animals were going to be difficult to deal with was at a county steer show when one of my half-ton 4-H steers escaped from our farm truck, chased me through the Gold Rush Junction theme park, now called Dollywood, ran me up a tree, and then head-butted the tree repeatedly trying to knock me out of it so he could kill me. I thought my life was over. I still get goose bumps when I think about it.

Only after I was rescued did I realize I'd saved myself by climbing a tree that had no limbs for the first ten feet! It had been like shinnying up a flagpole, but I was able to do it because it sure beat the alternative.

The second episode that made me question my vocation as a farmer happened when Dad was treating an infection in the rear hoof of a 1,000-pound Black Angus cow. He decided to use the task as an opportunity to teach me how to work on a cow safely, even when dealing with a difficult and sensitive area like a foot.

I had a bad feeling about it, but when Dad was in one of his instructional moods, all you could do was watch and listen. He put the big cow in a homemade holding chute at one end of our barn and then hollered for Mom to come and help him with his demonstration. Mom's name was Barbara, but everyone called her *Bob*. She was only five feet tall but she was quick to put Dad in his place whenever he needed it; and sometimes he really needed it.

As I watched Dad get ready, I realized he was going to be kneeling directly behind the cow, treating an infected and sore foot. Rather than taking the normal precaution of placing a two-by-four board behind the animal's rear legs to block its kicks, Dad decided to rely on an alternative safety method. He should've known better. He already had a crack in his skull from a cow kicking him when he was young.

He took hold of the cow's tail and arched it over her back in a crescent shape, saying to Mom, "Hold the tail like this, Bob."

Mom and I glanced at each other, both of us thinking, *Here we go again.*

Mom gamely took hold of the cow's tail and held it arched backwards over the cow's rump. "Now she can't kick," Dad said, "because her kicking nerve is pinched. But whatever you do, don't let go. If you let go, someone could get hurt."

My bad feelings about the situation intensified. Mom and I exchanged worried glances as Dad squatted down close behind the cow's back legs. "Dad," I said, "shouldn't you put somethin behind that cow's legs so she won't kick you?"

"Son," he said, "You just watch and learn. I've handled cows this way a hundred times!" Dad looked toward Mom, and said, "Now Bob, you keep that tail curled like I showed you."

She nodded to indicate her readiness.

When Dad took hold of the cow's back foot, the normally peaceful and friendly cow started dancing around in the holding chute. "Bob," Dad said, "hold that tail!"

Gradually, the cow settled down as Dad worked on her hoof. A couple of minutes later though, I noticed her back was bowing up sharply, as if she was straining for some reason. "Dad!" I yelled. "Look out!"

Dad glanced up to see what I was hollering about at the same instant a thick stream of bright green, semi-liquid manure came spewing from the cow's rear end. It blasted him right in the face. He sputtered and spit and swiped at the mess. Mom and I couldn't help it, we got to laughing so hard, both of us had to sit down.

Unfortunately this meant Mom let go of the cow's tail, so the cow followed up her bowel movement by kicking Dad in the chest, sending him flying backwards in a high speed somersault. Dad certainly gave me an unforgettable lesson that day about handling farm animals, but it wasn't the one he'd intended.

The third and final strike against my plan to be a cow farmer arrived in the form of a prolapsed uterus. This is a serious medical problem that occurs after a calf is born. The cow's uterus gets expelled, turned almost inside out, from the force of her pushing strongly during the calving process. It happened to one of Dad's cows in a pasture near a creek on a bitterly cold and windy January night. The calf was healthy and ready for mom to stand up so he could get his first meal, but we had some work to do to her before Junior could fill his belly.

The cow was still lying down from giving birth. To get into position behind her, I had to lie on my side on the wet, cold, muddy ground. It was extremely hard work, and not very pleasant, but after several attempts I eventually got the bloody uterus pushed back into place. Before I had time to get up, though, she began straining and out came everything again. What a mess.

I felt sorry for the helpless and suffering cow. We couldn't leave her like that. The expelled tissue would become necrotic and she'd get an infection and die a painful death. So, somehow, I had to do it all again.

For a second time, I got back into position and worked feverishly to stuff everything back where it belonged, and eventually I was successful. This time Dad and I quickly sewed up the opening so everything would stay where it should. It worked. The cow stood up and the newborn calf was now happily nursing.

This was the filthiest and most miserable situation I'd ever been in in my life. I sat in the mud in the open field, trying to wipe all the animal goo off myself. I looked up at the beautiful starry sky and thought, *There's gotta be an easier way to make a living.*

The next day I went to the university registrar's office and changed my major from Animal Science to Wildlife and Fisheries Science. Wild animals were bound to be easier to work with than cows, or at least that was my I thought at the time.

If I'd only known.

BEAR IN THE BACK SEAT

"YOU'RE GONNA GET US KILLED!" the helicopter pilot shouted. He couldn't believe the bear he was supposed to transport wasn't in a cage.

I stood next to where the sedated bear lay in a great lump of black fur and hollered back so he could hear me over the roar of the engine, "The bear's asleep!"

"Look at the claws on that thing! The teeth!" he said. "You should at least tie it up!"

"With what?" I said. "I don't have anything to tie her up with." The pilot was dumbfounded. "Don't worry," I shouted. "She won't wake up."

I tried to act confident. I figured the bear would remain asleep for at least a few more minutes, although, by this time, I couldn't remember exactly how long she'd been out. I was hesitant to give her another shot of the immobilization drugs because there was a very real chance I could kill her by keeping her asleep too long.

I had to figure out a way to reassure the pilot though, because I needed him to get us off the mountain. He had a good point. It wasn't the wisest thing in the world for me to put a large, un-restrained wild bear right behind his seat, especially since I can't always predict when the drugs will begin to wear off. But it wasn't my fault he'd showed up late.

I wondered why in the world a pilot who was terrified of bears had responded to a call to pick one up and transport it, but then I had to admit to myself that even though I was extremely nervous about helicopters, I'd called one to come pick me up. The pilot and I made quite a pair, both frightened and shouting at each other across the body of the unconscious bear.

Unfortunately there was no good alternative to the flight. If I couldn't relocate this bear, I'd have to put her down, euthanize her, and I didn't want to do that. She wasn't a bad bear. But she had to be moved to a less populated area for the safety of both Park visitors and the bear.

My job as Supervisory Wildlife Biologist was to protect people and animals, in that order. It's tough enough to manage wildlife in 520,000 acres of mountainous Park wilderness sandwiched between another 640,000 acres of national forest. It's even tougher when your territory contains the world's largest concentration of naïve tourists in close proximity to one of the country's densest concentrations of wild black bears.

The Great Smoky Mountains National Park is the most popular national park in the country. Nine million people visit every year and some of them come with the express intention of trying to get as close as possible to at least one of our 1,600 wild bears. It is a recipe for disaster.

I felt like a referee in the wild. My job was never what you'd call *easy*, but this helicopter ride was a spectacularly bad situation, even for me. And we hadn't even taken off yet.

We couldn't take off. That was part of the problem.

When you're working in a wilderness setting with wild animals that you're trying to keep wild, you can plan all you want, but something unanticipated will always happen. That's just the way it is.

This helicopter fiasco started because we had a problem bear at Silers Bald. Insensitive hikers had taught the bear some bad habits. It wasn't the bear's fault. So, rather than killing the bear, which I sure would've hated to do, I wanted to relocate her far away from people.

This was an effective strategy for dealing with most panhandling or nuisance bears. They weren't bad animals. It was just that they preferred to get their meals the easiest way possible, as most bears do. And if that was by bumming food from hikers, they'd do it.

The Appalachian Trail could be like a fast food drive-thru for a panhandling bear who'd lost its fear of humans. All the bear had to do was wait beside the trail and step out whenever people with food walked by. For dessert, he could visit the people who camped at Silers Bald shelter or any other backcountry camping area.

This bear's territory was about four miles from Clingmans Dome. Because of the extremely remote location where she was active, we needed a helicopter to move her. We didn't have enough time or people to carry her out on a wheeled litter. Plus, keeping her asleep during the long walk out would require that we give her a large amount of tranquilizer. That big a dose and the prolonged time under the effects of the drugs could kill her.

It's a steep climb out of Silers Bald over Mt. Buckley. Lugging a 175-pound bear along a narrow trail across uneven ground can get people hurt. It's extremely awkward, to say the least. We'd carried a bear out from Siler's Bald before, but it died before we made it. I sure didn't want that to happen again.

I was especially wary about having to ride in a helicopter because the company we used had crashed one in the Park when they were hauling materials from Mt. Le Conte. The load they'd been hauling had been a lot heavier, but at least it was inanimate.

I don't mind flying in big planes, but I'm not crazy about small ones. And helicopters make me *very* nervous. On a good day they scare me—on a day like this, with high winds, helicopters terrify me.

Nevertheless, I hiked up to Silers Bald and waited at the shelter hoping to see the bear. I didn't have to wait long. When I saw her, I called Dispatch and said, "She's here now. Is the helicopter ready to go?"

It was, so I got the capture dart ready. I shot the bear in the hip and she went down in five minutes. It took another thirty minutes for me to carry her from the shelter up to the small landing zone at the top of the ridge on Silers Bald.

I went ahead and called for the helicopter to come immediately because I didn't want to keep her asleep any longer than necessary. The longer the bear was down, the higher the risk she'd die. Dispatch called me back and said the helicopter would be there shortly.

On Silers Bald there's not a real clear place to land. There are lots of shrubs and small trees. When I got up there, I looked around and quickly became even more concerned. This wasn't good. There was so much tall vegetation I was afraid the helicopter's tail rotor would hit the brush and damage it either during landing or takeoff.

Atop the ridge, the wind was howling. That wasn't good either, but there was nothing I could do about it, so I hunkered down next to the sleeping bear and waited.

Eventually the helicopter showed up, but it took a lot longer than thirty minutes. By the time it arrived the bear had already been asleep for over an hour. Then the pilot took his time landing.

I watched the helicopter hover as the pilot tried to find a place to set down. After several tries, the chopper finally landed and the pilot got out, but he didn't come to help me load the bear. Instead he went to the back door on his side of the helicopter and started fiddling with it.

I walked around to tell him that I'd need help lifting the bear into the helicopter, but before I could say anything, he said, "Help me take these back doors off."

I thought, *Take the doors off?*

"We don't need to take the doors off to the get the bear in," I said. "She'll easily fit in the back seat."

"I'm not worried about getting the bear *in*," he yelled, "I'm worried about how fast you can get it *out* if it wakes up during the flight."

"I'm not planning for her to wake up during the flight," I said. "Don't worry."

The pilot shot me a look that said, *I've heard about you and your wild animals.* Of course I'd heard about him and his crash, too, but I tried not to let it show.

"Well," he said, "we're taking both rear doors off before the bear gets in."

"What's your thinking?" I asked.

"My thinking is that if this bear wakes up, she's gotta have somewhere to go."

"Where do you expect her to go?" I asked.

"Out the door instead of into the front seat!"

"I don't know if I can get a bear to jump out of a helicopter," I admitted. I meant it both as a matter of principle and as a practical issue.

I had no idea how I was supposed to wrestle with a bear in the backseat of a helicopter. It wasn't like playing with your brother across a car seat during a family vacation.

"We can't afford to let the bear wake up while we're in the air," the pilot said as he tucked the door into a small storage area in the back of the chopper. I thought to myself, *You're telling me.*

"It won't come to that," I said, faking as much confidence as possible. I could only pray that I was right. Even if I could somehow manage it, it would be horrible to force a bear to leap out of a helicopter in mid-flight. What a tragedy, it would be a nightmare.

"How will you know if she's waking up?" the pilot asked as he helped me position the bear in the space behind our seats.

"She won't," I said. At least I hoped she wouldn't.

"But what if she does?" he asked, as we went to climb inside.

"I'll handle it, trust me!" I said. "If she wakes up, it'll happen slowly. I can probably hold her down long enough for you to land or I can give her more drugs that'll put her back to sleep.

"Promise you won't let her get up front with me," the pilot said, nearly hysterical.

"Don't you worry about the bear," I said, "you just keep your eyes on the road and get us off this mountain in one piece." As I spoke, one of the capricious gusts of wind blew my National Park Service hat off and it landed in the top of a tree. We both stared at it. It wasn't a good omen.

We climbed into the helicopter and fastened our seatbelts, but the pilot didn't make any move to takeoff. He sat staring over his shoulder, grimacing at the large lump of smelly black fur behind our seats. Bears have a very strong odor.

"Please, please, *please*," I said, "you just fly the helicopter and let me worry about the bear!"

He shook his head slowly.

We were sitting side by side. He was on the left and I was on the right. We were both worried about each other's competence. Both of our lives literally depended on each other's expertise and skill at doing our jobs. I knew I was bluffing, so I figured he probably was, too. It's sort of funny now, but it wasn't at the time.

The pilot was clearly upset, but he faced forward and revved the engine. The chopper began to shake violently but it didn't lift off the ground. Now that the pilot was facing forward, focused on flying, I turned around and flicked the bear's ear to test her responsiveness. It might've twitched a little, which is an early sign that she was waking up, but I really couldn't be sure on account of all the vibration and the wind.

I began to get a sick feeling in my stomach.

The pilot shouted and pointed as he shared his strategy for dealing with the violent winds. "We're gonna lift off, then turn straight into the wind, and fly over the mountain into Tennessee." At least that was his plan.

He revved the throttle, giving it everything he had. The whirling blades were whipping bits of leaves and grass into a frenzy around us, but the helicopter still wouldn't lift off. Instead it shuddered violently and remained in place.

The good news was that we were on a bald, one of the rare patches of the Smokies that wasn't heavily forested, so there was at least a small area to maneuver in. The bad news was that we were nearly surrounded by an impenetrable thicket of leucothe shrubs. The locals called them *dog hobble* and *witch hobble*. And they were called that for a good reason.

If neither a dog nor a witch could get through the bushes, I was pretty sure the helicopter wouldn't make it either, even with the aid of the violent winds howling around us. But instead of concentrating on the difficult task facing him, taking off from a confined space during a hillbilly hurricane, the pilot kept looking over his shoulder at the bear.

"Why aren't we taking off?" I shouted.

"Downdraft!" he yelled.

I looked out at the spectacular view. The endless corrugations of blue, interspersed with fluffy white clouds looked so peaceful. But looks were deceiving. The wind was invisible. In another situation it would've felt like paradise. But right now it was sort of the opposite. It seemed like the hand of God was holding us down, saying, *Not just yet*. Or maybe it was the hand of the Devil.

The Cherokee nickname for the strange bald areas was *Satan's Footprints*. Scientists couldn't figure out why these odd treeless patches inexplicably appeared in one of the densest forests on earth, an area so biologically diverse that it was designated as a world environmental treasure by the United Nations.

This particular area was famous for wicked whimsical wind shears over a hundred miles an hour. The savage gusts, called orographic lifts, had caused many airplane and helicopter crashes. Several of them had been fatal. I worked with two rangers who'd been in helicopter crashes. One of them was partially disabled for the rest of his life.

So far none of the crashes had been caused by a bear, but there was always a first time for everything. Normally, when large wild animals were transported by helicopter, they were carried in a net suspended by a long rope in a *sling load*. But not this time.

I was beginning to realize I should've used a net that would dangle a hundred feet below the helicopter, but it was too late for that now. Now, more than anything, I wanted the pilot to concentrate on his job so I could concentrate on mine.

The noise and vibration of the chopper was deafening. If we didn't lift off soon, the engine sounded like it would explode. Either way, the racket and violent jarring could rouse the bear any minute. But I didn't dare give her another dose of tranquilizer yet. If I overdosed her and she died, all this trouble would be for nothing.

The pilot looked over his shoulder yet again, eyes wide with terror, and I bellowed, "*Forget about the bear*! *You* fly the helicopter! *I'll* handle the bear!"

To be honest I had no idea how I was going to manage the bear if she woke up. I didn't have a Plan B. The big girl had lost her fear of humans and had become a problem by panhandling. She had to leave the area one way or another.

Hikers had fed her for fun through the chain link fence on the shelter or they'd carelessly stored food or garbage where she could get to it, foolishly teaching her to associate humans with food. So she'd been approaching people in the area looking for an easy meal from whatever they were packing. Her bad behavior was the result of training by insensitive hikers.

So far she hadn't hurt anyone, but it was potentially a very dangerous situation for both hikers and the bear. Unless you have strong nerves and some understanding of bears, a bear chasing you because it hopes you'll throw down your granola bar can be hard to differentiate from a bear chasing you because it hopes to kill you and eat you for supper.

I'd decided the best strategy for this bear was to move her to a less populated area at least forty miles away where she could live out her life in peace, safely away from a high concentration of hikers and campers. Fortunately, some bears can usually be managed this way. Tourists, on the other hand, are often impossible to deal with.

You can ask visitors to not feed the bears, beg them to stop, explain they're killing the bear if they feed it. You can threaten them, write tickets, and fine them. For some, you can even confiscate their vehicle and put them in jail, but certain people on vacation are living purely for the moment and they won't listen. It was for these few inconsiderate or crazy people that I was risking my life, the pilot's, and the bear's.

The pilot and I exchanged worried glances. It was obvious he thought something bad was about to happen—and I did too, except I knew he thought we were going to be bitten, clawed, and mauled to death, while I was pretty sure we'd crash and burn before the bear would have a chance to hurt us.

Then suddenly the helicopter lifted far enough off the ground to become airborne. And the instant it did, a brutal gust of wind caught it and tossed it like a bit of dandelion fluff. *Holy Smoke! I'm too young to die*, I thought as we blew sideways.

We were now flying, finally, but were gyrating wildly and going in the wrong direction. We barely cleared the shrubs on the edge of the bald and then, in a flash, there was nothing but a very long drop underneath us as we zipped past the bluffs at the edge of the bald.

The helicopter was shooting sideways at warp speed into North Carolina. I didn't know much about our route, but I knew enough to be certain we were moving away from Tennessee.

"We're goin the wrong way!" I shouted.

"This is the *only* way we *can* go in this wind!" yelled the pilot.

Both of us were painfully aware that we needed to get to our landing spot in Tennessee as soon as possible. The pilot twisted in his seat to take another look at the bear. I saw him do it and threw my hands in the air. "Keep your eyes on the road!" I hollered.

He acted like he didn't hear me, so I screamed, "Don't worry about the bear!"

He shot me a dirty look and stoically turned to face forward. Then gradually, like a sea captain navigating his ship during a terrible storm, he was able to maneuver the helicopter toward Gatlinburg. I was never so grateful in my life as when we landed in the parking lot of Gatlinburg High School. It was all I could do not to fling myself out of the helicopter and kiss the ground.

A wildlife technician was waiting for us with a transfer cage and as soon as we touched down he ran over and helped me unload the bear. The instant we pulled the bear clear of the helicopter, the pilot lifted off with only a slight wave. I think he was happy to get away from the bear and from me.

The bear wasn't completely asleep any more, but she was still groggy and sluggish enough that we were able to load her into the transfer cage and slam the door before she bit anyone. We'd made it, but just barely. I'd cut this one *way* too close.

We released the bear in her new home and never heard of her causing any more problems. The decision to move her was the right one. I'm not sure what helicopter pilots make, but I think my pilot that day felt he deserved a raise or at least a bonus. I felt the same.

.

THE BEAR WHISPERER

I WAS YOUNG AND DUMB, just twenty-three years old, when I was first hired to work in the Park. It was 1978 and I'd heard they were looking for wild hog managers. It was a seasonal job and the pay was not too good, but it sounded exciting to me.

At the time there was no book to read, no school where you could go, to learn how to handle wild hogs, bear, elk, deer, wolves, otters, falcons, and other wild critters, especially when you added people into the mix. The Park wasn't a zoo, although some naïve visitors thought it was. There were no cages or fences to keep the animals in or out. Rangers had to deal with wild animals the best they could. Nobody else was managing these kinds of large wild animals, at least not on the scale of the Great Smoky Mountains National Park.

One of the perennial problems in the Smokies during the 1970s was the exploding population of wild hogs. They aren't native to the area. These wild pigs are a cross between free-ranging domestic hogs and massive, wary Russian wild boars imported by a wealthy businessman for his private hunting lodge on Hoopers Bald, North Carolina in 1912.

The beasts escaped, of course, and their hybridized descendants are amazing looking creatures with huge front shoulders and tiny back ends, called *Rooshins* by the locals. They're shrewd animals who plow up the Park with their razor sharp tusks, eating everything in sight including rare flower bulbs, leaving behind an unbelievable mess and very little food for the other critters.

There aren't many positive things to say about these pigs in the wild, so I didn't mind helping reduce their numbers inside the Park. What I didn't know was that the National Park Service employees, most of whom were not local people and definitely not hunters, didn't have the necessary skills and experience to run their new wild hog eradication program.

To get an experienced person, they had to hire one of the most notorious poachers in the area. The guy they hired was a hard core expert in dealing with the prolific wild hogs that lived in the Smokies.

A poacher was perfect for the job of hog hunter because when the government said *manage* they actually meant *exterminate*. Buck Branham, a hard-working mountain man and woodsman, was hired. He became responsible for supervising and training his first official assistant hog hunter—me.

I'd been around all kinds of animals since my earliest childhood. I'd worked with mules in the fields, owned a horse, showed beef cattle through 4-H and Future Farmers of America, and helped raise pigs and chickens on our farm.

I'd also been a hunter my entire life, so I knew a fair amount about the area and the local wildlife. I thought I probably knew as much as most people about handling large animals, and I was right. But that was only true because, back then, hardly anything was known about using science in handling and managing large free-ranging wild animals in the mountains.

I didn't get much of a training program. Buck simply handed me a shotgun and a backpack and threw me into the deep end of the Park. Soon after I was hired, he told me I'd have to go into the backcountry and stay there for the entire summer. The *backcountry* was the vast wilderness area of the Park that wasn't close to a road or accessible by a motorized vehicle. Most of it was very rough terrain that you could get to only by way of the 800 miles of rocky, dirt hiking trails that snaked through the Park.

The idea worried me. I'd never spent one night in the Park, much less in the backcountry. I thought I was going to have to go live in the middle of the 800 square miles of steep jungle-like wilderness of the Great Smoky Mountains National Park *by myself* for the whole summer.

This turned out to not be true. Buck was just trying to scare me, and he succeeded. "I'll haul supplies back and forth to you," he told me. He didn't say how often these deliveries would occur and I was too proud to ask. So, the very next day, on a beautiful morning, I found myself out there in the middle of the woods, alone, roaming around with a shotgun, looking for the elusive and destructive wild hogs.

On an evening soon afterwards, at dusk, I was operating out of Gregory Bald, wandering around between Parsons Bald and Backcountry Campsite #13, Sheep Pen Gap, when I saw a white-tailed deer run across the trail with a huge black bear chasing it.

I foolishly decided it would be fun to blow at the bear and distract him and save the deer. A series of high-pitched blowing sounds is the alarm sound deer make. That's how they warn each other of danger. So I imitated the deer's danger signal thinking it would confuse the bear.

I was right, it did get the bear's attention. Almost immediately I realized my mistake. Bears associate the blowing sound with deer. This bear was looking for supper and now he thought he had more than one choice. To a bear's way of thinking, one deer's as good as another. And a deer that wasn't moving made for a much easier meal than a deer that was running away at top speed.

My stupid joke had the effect of saving the deer. But it also caused the bear to look my way and then start heading straight for me. The bear raised his head, slowly moving it back and forth, sniffing the air, trying to get my scent.

A bear's eyesight isn't that great. At that distance, he couldn't make out what I was by looking at me. Their sense of smell is excellent, but unfortunately I was downwind from the bear. That wasn't good.

I began to get scared. I had a shotgun, but I didn't want to have to use it. I was supposed to kill hogs, not bears. This was my first close encounter with the famous icon of the Smokies and I certainly didn't want the bear to end up dead.

Bears are the symbol of the Great Smoky Mountains National Park. They're very near and dear to millions of visitors, and to me, too. Having to kill one of them to save myself on my first overnight trip in the backcountry would be a disaster for the bear and for my career. So, I did the only thing I could think of, I started talking to the bear and apologizing.

"Bear, it's me," I said. "I shouldn't have done what I did, I'mmm sorry."

But the bear kept coming. He didn't even break stride. He was moving toward me through tall weeds, so I could only see his head. The wind was blowing in my face, so I knew he couldn't smell me at all. As far as the bear knew, I presented no danger, and was a very large, dumb, slow-moving snack.

I talked louder and louder as the bear came closer. Even today, more than thirty years later, I still get chill bumps thinking about that big bear coming toward me. He popped out of the waist-high vegetation onto the trail about ten yards from where I was standing. By this time I was hollering at the top of my lungs. "Bear! Bear! Get back bear!" But the bear continued to come toward me.

I was walking backwards slowly, shouting over and over, "Bear! Bear! Get back bear!" The bear came to within three or four feet of me. He was out of the weeds now so I could see all of him. He looked like he'd weigh over 300 pounds. Of course, I wasn't spending much time guessing his weight. All I could think about was that he was big, black, and ready to attack.

Even though he was walking on all fours, his head came up above my waist. He stood there facing me, with his head panning back and forth, trying to catch my scent. He was still trying to figure out what I was. Not knowing anything else to do, I fired the shotgun into the air, twice.

The bear immediately stopped moving and stared at me for what seemed like an hour, but was only about five seconds. I was shaking all over and my knees were knocking. Then the bear bobbed his head a couple of times, turned, and *slowly* walked back into the vegetation until he was out of sight. I continued to walk backwards, watching intently as the distance increased between me and the bear, until I felt safe again.

That's as close as I ever came to messing in my britches. I'd learned my first and best lesson about bears that day. I found out that it was extremely dangerous to do *anything* that made a bear associate you with food.

Since then I've learned that some bear hunters will imitate a deer fawn in distress to lure a bear to their location. Well, not me. I'm through having a conversation with any bear that's actively searching for food.

For the rest of that day and for a long time afterwards I wasn't sure if I was in the right job. I wondered what I'd gotten myself into. Clearly I had a lot to learn about dealing with bears.

But experience is the best teacher, and after a while I gradually stopped being so nervous around bears in the wild. I realized that the scary situation had been my own fault. I learned that I didn't have to be so intimidated by bears, but I certainly needed to respect them.

In the coming decades, I'd get a lot of experience that demonstrated what a fine line that could be.

Not only was I lucky enough to be protected from the consequences of my foolishness in those early days, but I seemed to have gotten the job by divine intervention.

The mountains dominated the skyline to the southeast of my home in Seymour, Tennessee, but because I lived and worked on a farm in a rural area, I had all the room I could ever want. I didn't have any urge to drive a few miles to a place I could see from my house. I'd never even gone into the Park before except to swim a few times after church on Sunday afternoons in the big swimming hole near the Park's Gatlinburg entrance.

But now that I was in college and looking for a summer job, I sent in an application for a seasonal job at the Park. Then I followed it up by driving to Headquarters to see if I could find anyone to talk to in person.

I was taken to Mike Myers' office where I found him sitting behind a desk shuffling through huge stacks of paper. I introduced myself and he said, "Wow, that's interesting. I just finished reading your application and here you come walking in the door!"

Mike was looking for someone to hunt pigs. I hadn't realized such a job existed, but was very fortunate and got hired. The whole thing was a miracle, a blessing from God. I couldn't believe it. It was so exciting. I loved the outdoors and enjoyed working with animals and now I was going to get paid for it! The pay wasn't much, but the experiences and adventures were going to be priceless.

BLINDED BY THE LIGHT

THE FIRST FEW TIMES I was sent into the backcountry, by the end of the week my body felt like it did on the morning after a high school football game. My thighs, calves, back, feet, and shoulders were very sore. Gradually I became stronger and got in better condition, but, at first, it was tough.

Part of the difficulty was all the walking I had to do on the steep mountain trails carrying a week's worth of food, clothing, camping gear, shotgun, battery, light, and shells. When you work in the backcountry you have to walk all the time. Trucks, ATVs, and dirt bikes are not allowed there. So, anywhere you want to go, for everything you need to do, you have to walk.

Even though I was young and in fairly good shape, I'd get short of breath as I trudged uphill. My clothes were always soaked with sweat by the time I reached the top of the mountain. When I tried to sleep my muscles would get tighter than a banjo string and my legs would cramp.

The good thing about being totally exhausted though, is that it usually helped me go to sleep. I had to get really tired every day or I couldn't go to sleep in my tent at night because there were so many mysterious sounds outside my tent. But, if I was tired enough, I could go to sleep no matter what noises I heard.

I never admitted to Buck the dumb mistake I'd made tricking the bear into thinking I was a deer. I didn't need to. After watching me stumble and bumble around in the woods for a few weeks he took pity on me and decided I needed some on-the-job training.

Anybody would've needed help learning to hunt wild hogs in the mountainous terrain. They're active mainly at night and they're extremely elusive. Lucky for me, Buck had a lot of experience. He'd been doing unofficial hog control in the Park for many years.

It was a source of great amusement in certain local circles that the National Park Service was now *paying* the most notorious poacher in the area to teach them how to hunt hogs. It was thought to be hilarious that they'd been forced to politely request the services of a poacher and make him a government employee with full benefits. But the Park Service knew the damage that wild hogs caused, so they did it anyway. In 1977 Buck was hired as a government hog hunter, a.k.a., paid poacher.

Buck's whole family lived right outside the Park boundary. He was the kind of guy who could make it just fine in the wilderness with only a can of beanee weenee, a knife, a piece of rope, a small tarp, a flashlight, and a pack of matches. He came from the vanishing breed of *real* mountain people. He could live off the land and survive. His idea of real luxury on a camping trip was to bring some cookies made by his wife, Lois, who he referred to as the *Ole Lady*.

Not all of the Park Service strategies worked as well as hiring Buck. Soon after they hired him, they tried issuing a contract to a Georgia hog hunter and paid him to come in and hunt hogs in North Carolina, but it blew up in their faces. There were a *lot* of local hunters who would've *loved* to hunt there for free.

When the Georgia fellow came, the local hunters went ballistic. Some of them set up a roadblock on Hwy. 129 to try and stop him from getting into the Park. National Park Service boats wouldn't run because someone had put sugar into the gas tanks. People threatened to burn down buildings at Hazel Creek, one of the main drainages flowing into Fontana Lake on the North Carolina side of the Park.

Buck tried to work with the Georgia hunter and the hog dogs he'd brought with him. He watched them run pigs all over the place. But, the project was a dismal failure. At the end of the day, they managed to catch only one small pig, and Buck did that. More importantly, the contract with someone from out-of-state generated long-lasting hard feelings from the locals. The government had to admit defeat and send the Georgia hog hunter home.

The Park Service needed a different strategy to get rid of the wild pigs, so they decided to hire seasonal hog hunters, starting in 1978. That's when my job as a wildlife ranger began.

Buck, my boss, was in his fifties when I started. That was more than twice my age, so he seemed very old to me at the time. He bought the guns and traps, designed any specialized equipment we needed, and came up with our hog-catching tactics.

For good or bad, he was my instructor. Unfortunately, my job almost ended with my first training session.

It was night when Buck drove me three miles up a steep, narrow, rocky road in a worn out old CJ5 Jeep, then we continued on foot to the area where he wanted to teach me how to hunt hogs.

We were on the Meigs Mountain Trail, between Metcalf Bottoms and Tremont. We didn't have any fancy equipment. We had only mercury-activated lights attached to our Model 870 12-gauge shotguns in a precarious system he'd rigged using six-volt bulbs powered by twelve-volt batteries.

The homemade lights were certainly bright, but because we were using twice as much power as we should've been, sometimes the bulbs would explode when you turned them on.

Buck and I were walking along a trail in the dark, with me in the front, when we heard pigs rooting, squealing, and grunting nearby. It sounded like they were just up ahead on the trail, slowly working their way in our direction.

Buck and I stopped momentarily to make a plan. "You get the

ones on left," he whispered, "and I'll get the ones on right."

I was trying to hide it, but I was a little afraid of wild hogs. I'd heard countless stories about how mean they were, and how smart. And I'd seen the trophies hunters made of their long, curved, razor-sharp tusks, called *tushes* in the local dialect.

I knew *tush hogs*, as they're called in the Smokies, had killed people and animals of all sizes, including a lot of famous warriors in history, even well-armed noblemen and kings. So there was no doubt in my mind that they could inflict a lot of damage on me.

As Buck and I were getting ready, the wild hogs were working their way closer to us. They made a lot of noise plowing through the dry leaves, grunting and clearing their noses by blowing dirt out of their snouts. There were intermittent high-pitched squeals as they competed with each other for acorns, grubs, or earthworms.

I realized that Buck was standing still for some reason, but it was so dark I couldn't tell what he was doing. "Buck," I whispered, "are you ready?"

He leaned toward me and whispered back, "Give me a minute, son."

We were standing about fifteen yards from the pigs, downwind of them, so they couldn't smell us. After a few more moments of fiddling in the dark, Buck said, "Yeah, I'm ready."

Then we both switched on our lights. They came on for one blinding second and then both of them blew out at the same time. Neither of us could see a thing.

It was a dark night and the flash of the over-powered lights had ruined whatever night vision we'd acquired up to that point. There had been only the tiniest chance that both our bulbs would blow out at the same time, but that's what happened.

I was totally blinded and I knew the hogs were coming toward us, so I quickly jumped back, trying to move out of their way. When I did, I slammed into Buck. He hadn't moved out of the way because he was calmly trying to put another bulb into the socket of his light.

I hit him hard enough to knock him down. And unfortunately we were standing on the edge of a steep bank, so he went flying downhill headfirst. All this chaotic movement happened while both of us were unable to see anything at all. Lucky for us, the pigs had been blinded by the flash, too.

Like any animal, wild hogs can be extremely aggressive when they're suddenly threatened by something nearby. So, even though they couldn't see, they attacked us as a group. The whole herd ran straight toward where the bright light flashes had come from.

The blind were attacking the blind.

The herd of pigs stampeded by me in the dark, making loud sounds, snuffling and grunting and squealing, as they rushed past my legs. I was leaping around randomly, hoping somehow to get away from them.

It was pitch black. I could feel things brushing against my legs, hogs racing by at top speed, but I had no way to avoid them. One hog ran right between my legs and kept going! It was chaos.

After the gang of hogs rushed past me, they continued stampeding on a trajectory that took them right over the top of Buck. He was sprawled on the ground, head downhill, feet up in the air, with no way to avoid getting tap-danced on by the pigs.

He was hollering and cursing at the Rooshins and they were grunting and snorting back at him. Most of the herd trampled right across the top of him. When it seemed like they were gone, I said, "Buck? You okay?"

He didn't answer. I carefully made my way down the bank and

helped him get turned the right way on the hillside so he could sit up and then stand. Then I walked him back up the hill and onto the trail. By then we were getting a little of our night vision back.

Buck was bruised and scraped and dirty from the fall and from where the pigs had run him over. He even smelled like a pig and that wasn't good. He had hoof prints scattered across the front of his National Park Service uniform.

When the stampede started, I was sure one or both of us was going to get hurt bad, but somehow neither of us did. I apologized to Buck as he dusted himself off. But he wasn't having any of it. "Son," he said, "next time why don't you just go ahead and *shoot* me."

I tried not to stare at the hoof prints the Rooshins had left across his shirt. I felt they were my fault. I paid for it, though. That night turned out to be the beginning, and the end, of my training from Buck.

DREAMING OF BEARS

I USED TO BE AFRAID of bears. I'd never been around them before and didn't know what to expect. When I first started working in the Park I was nervous about bears, wild hogs, and staying in the backcountry. I didn't know what to expect. That meant I was frequently worried while I was doing my job. Thank goodness I learned a lot over the years and came to realize you don't need to be afraid, just extremely cautious.

When you're working in the backcountry, you're mostly by yourself. You can't help having some concerns about bears, hogs, and the dark. You worry about what's around the next curve in the trail. You wonder if something's following you, or what it was that made a weird sound. At times, you can get a little paranoid.

A few of the guys were afraid of the dark and would never hike very far away from their camp. The basic human fears never leave you, no matter how long you work in the wilderness. It's like walking through a haunted house or going on a haunted ride at the county fair. You know something's gonna jump out and scare the fool out of you sooner or later. You just don't know when.

When you hear something in the woods at night, it could be a bear, a wild boar, a squirrel, a person, or maybe just the wind. But you don't know for sure *what* it is.

At first a gun helped me feel a little more secure, but later, when I learned how animals behaved in the wild, I got to where I didn't need a gun to feel safe or to *be* safe.

If you spend enough years in the woods, eventually you come to know that nothing's gonna jump out and get you. Most wild animals have a survival instinct that tells them to stay away from people. It was more dangerous to drive my truck to work than it was to walk in the backcountry.

Unfortunately, though, from the first minute you get a job in the Park you start hearing horror stories. You get dire warnings from people you don't even know. You hear the kinds of things you've never heard before, even though you've lived a stone's throw from the Park all your life. Absolutely *everybody* tells you how dangerous it is out in the backcountry—rangers, people at the grocery store. Everyone you run into has a story about how dangerous it is.

But no matter how intimidated you are, you can't stay awake twenty-four hours a day for a week. Eventually you have to go to sleep and a gun won't help you at all if you're asleep.

At a site near Backcountry Campsite #13, Sheep Pen Gap, there was an old fuel drum we used as a storage cache. It was about fifteen yards from the tent site. The metal container had a sealable latch so animals couldn't open it. But bears could smell interesting smells coming from it, like trail mix, candy bars, and empty tuna cans, so they'd beat on it all night long.

It's hard to sleep when you can hear something like that going on right near where you're lying. One second all you can hear is the sound of crickets or maybe an owl, then a bear would start banging on the drum and sleeping was impossible.

It took me years to understand bears well enough to know that if a bear really wants to hurt you, you might as well say your farewells because they are extremely powerful creatures born with a natural expertise for catching their prey. Killing is part of their instinctive skill set. If a bear decides to attack you in a predatory way, you'd better understand exactly what's happening and respond appropriately, or you won't survive the encounter.

Bears are wild animals and can be dangerous due to their powerful teeth and jaws, and their claws that can flay you alive. They can rip through nine-gauge chain link fence or three-quarter-inch plywood. Bears are incredibly strong!

scratch.

Most bears have a natural reluctance to start a fight with a human, even one who is unconscious, or sleeping, or staying overnight in the backcountry. The bears figure it would be too risky to engage with a person.

Of course the bears might've left the fellow alone because it was a good year for berries and acorns and they had plenty of food in their bellies that day. That man was even luckier than any of us realized at the time, because he'd fainted just a couple of miles from where a hiker would be attacked and killed by bears a few years later.

If it had taken us longer to find him, the outcome might not have turned out as well.

THE OLD BEAR

ANIMALS DON'T LIVE FOREVER. Bears and elk don't live to be 150, or even fifty years old in the wild. They can sometimes have a difficult life in the mountains. When you see firsthand how harsh Mother Nature can be, it's really sobering. The Smoky Mountains are a tough place to make a living for any animal. A wildlife ranger gets a unique perspective on this.

Once I got a call in the middle of January. A bear in distress had been sighted near the Chimneys picnic area. I drove over and walked up the Chimneys Nature Trail until I found a huge old bear lying across the trail, faint with starvation. He was a very large-frame fellow, who was just skin and bones, a skeleton with fur over it, unable to go on.

He was clearly very near the end of his life. He'd used up all his fat reserves and had to come out of hibernation, out into the brutal cold, hoping to find something to eat. Obviously he'd not been able to gather enough food during the previous fall, so he didn't have enough fat on him to make it through the winter sleeping snug in his den.

But this time of year, the dead of winter, there was no easy food for him to find. He had so little energy that he couldn't even muster the strength to make it to the picnic area to look for scraps visitors had thrown on the ground.

When I found him, he was lying on the ground suffering, unable to get up. As I got close, all he could do was raise his head to look at me as if asking for my help.

It was a sad situation. Normally we don't see the end of the life of an old animal. Usually that takes place in a den or a remote location deep in the wilderness. But this old bear came out to a place where we were able to see what he was going through.

I decided to put him down humanely to prevent any further pain. It was the best thing I could do for him. Sometimes doing that is like being a Good Samaritan.

I felt sorry for him, but it was the right thing to do. We can't save a bear in this situation, It was simply his time. As I carefully injected the drug into the old bear, I wondered about all the things he had seen and experienced during his life. He looked back at me, then slowly lowered his head, closed his eyes, and went to sleep.

Nature is hard in many ways. Usually we're unaware of these sad situations that happen in the wild. I try to help the animals if I can, especially when they're in tough circumstances where they can't help themselves. It's certainly not pleasant, but it's merciful.

Sometimes I think about that diabetic man who thought he was dreaming when he saw the bears standing over him. I hope the old bear who saw me looking down at him thought the same thing. Nothing to be afraid of, it's all just a dream.

THE HITCHHIKER

EVERYONE HAS WEIRD DREAMS in the backcountry, including me, but every once in a while a person wakes up and realizes what they thought was a bad dream is actually real.

This happened to a fellow who was backpacking by himself. He was the sole camper at Backcountry Campsite #53, Poke Patch, on upper Deep Creek Trail. His trip was uneventful until dark when something suddenly woke him up from a sound sleep.

It was a bear patting the outside of his tent, searching to see what food, if any, the man might've brought into the backcountry with him. The bear pushed against the outside of the guy's tent hard enough to make it collapse on him. The fellow was unable to see what was going on or do anything about it.

Then the bear bit through the tent fabric, locked his jaws around the man's arm, and started dragging him across the campsite, tent and all. The fellow was tall, 6' 2", but the bear was easily able to drag him and the tent at will.

The man screamed and thrashed and struggled until he was able to punch the bear in the nose and make it let go of his arm. Then he managed to tear his way out of the mangled tent and escape. He let the bear keep the tent.

There were no other campers to get help from, so the fellow took off barefoot, wearing only his boxer shorts and socks, carrying a Bowie knife he managed to grab out of the jumble of his gear as he ran away. A few minutes later he realized that during his panicked run from the bear he'd gotten off the trail and was lost, so he wisely decided to stop where he was.

It was cold and raining, and he was pretty miserable standing around without his clothes, so he lay on the ground and buried himself in leaves to try to stay warm while he waited for daylight. At dawn he crawled out from under his pile of leaves and hiked uphill about four miles toward the Deep Creek trailhead along Hwy. 441, Newfound Gap Road, in North Carolina.

The last hundred yards of the trail before it intersects with the highway is an extremely steep climb. When he finally managed to pull himself up onto the road, the man was still traumatized from his encounter with the bear. He ran along Newfound Gap Road trying to flag someone down.

Unfortunately nobody would stop for a large, hysterical man who was covered in mud and leaves, wearing only a pair of boxer shorts, and brandishing a Bowie knife. It's hard to blame them.

First impressions are hard to overcome and clothes apparently do make the man, because the Park Service got several calls about a filthy, crazed man in his underwear standing in the middle of Hwy. 441 waving a big knife.

Not a single person was going to stop to help a guy like that, so a couple of North Carolina rangers went out and picked him up. When they got to him he was still in shock. They managed to get him settled down and we found out what happened. Once we learned about the incident, one of our best guys, Chuck Hester, was sent into the backcountry along with a wildlife intern, Robert Fey. They went to the campsite to see if they could locate the bear.

Poke Patch backcountry campsite is the upper reaches of Deep Creek which flows to Bryson City, North Carolina. It's near a popular trout fishing spot, and traditionally local people fished there in early springtime, so there would've been a lot of cleaning and frying of fish going on in the area. The smells of cooking would've been very attractive to a bear.

Chuck and Robert set up two tents—one with an electric fence around it that they intended to sleep in and another one, what we call a *dummy tent*, with no fence, that they used to simulate a backpacker's camp.

The plan was that the rogue bear would go for the unprotected tent and the rangers would hear him and come out of their safely-fenced area and capture the bear with a tranquilizer dart. Then, based on the behavior of the bear, we could make the right decision about what to do with it.

When Chuck and Robert got everything set up it was nearly dark. Robert had just gone into the protected tent and lay down to doze while they waited to see if a bear would show up. Chuck was taking the first shift, stationed near the dummy tent waiting with both a dart rifle and a high-powered conventional rifle.

Soon after everything was set up, a fairly large bear came boldly into the area, but things didn't go according to plan. There was no activity at the dummy tent, but all of a sudden Chuck heard a ruckus from the tent where Robert was lying down. Chuck shined his spotlight up the hill and saw Robert hurtling toward him in his sock feet screaming, "Ba-Ba-Ba-Ba-Ba-Ba-Ba-Bearrrrrrrrrrr!"

Unbeknownst to Chuck, the bear had walked up to the tent where Robert was, knocked the electric fence down, and swatted the tent, sending Robert running and yelling. Chuck ran up the hill and was able to dart the bear. Then, with the animal in hand, Chuck contacted Dispatch by radio, and they in turn called me by phone. There was a discussion and Chuck was advised to put the animal down.

It was a sad situation, but in light of the bear's direct attack on two people in tents it was decided the animal should be euthanized immediately. Sometimes it's a tough call, making sure you have the right bear before you take such serious action, but because this bear went after Robert in the protected tent first, we were very confident we had the right bear.

In the Smokies it's very unusual for a bear to attack a tent with someone in it, so in light of the location and style of aggression, we knew this was the same animal that had attacked the camper. It's pitiful, but the truth is, if that bear had never been able to bum any food or scavenge any fish scraps carelessly left around a campsite, he'd probably never have learned to associate humans with food.

If campers had been more careful with their food and scraps, that hiker would've been able to have a pleasant sojourn in the Park and the bear would've been able to live out the rest of its life in the wild. But some earlier hikers and campers didn't follow the rules. They just don't get the big picture. So we had a tragedy, almost two tragedies, over something so simple, so easy to avoid.

This is the second most important lesson about bears. Don't ever feed a bear anything and don't ever leave any food scraps behind when you're visiting the Park.

If you care about the bears at all, if you want other people to be able to have safe visits to the Park, dispose of your garbage in bear-proof containers or carry out all your food, scraps, and garbage when you leave. Pack it in, pack it out. The Park endlessly preaches *Leave No Trace*, but some people just won't listen.

To this day, that bear's skull sits in the wildlife office at Park Headquarters. We use it as a teaching tool so people will understand what happens when they don't follow the rules. The bear nearly always comes out on the short end of the stick.

When I think of that wild looking hitchhiker standing alongside the road in his underwear waving a big knife, trying to catch a ride to a ranger station, I can't help but marvel at the difference clothes, time of day, and the political climate can make.

When I first started out with the Park Service, it was such a long commute from Headquarters to get to the Gregory Bald trailheads in the western reaches of the Park, I used to drive my personal vehicle to the end of Forge Creek Turnaround and then hitchhike to Sam's Gap on Parson's Branch Road. That way I could shorten my drive and save gas.

I'd stand beside the road in my ranger uniform holding a shotgun and tourists would stop and offer me a ride. Of course that would never be allowed nowadays and it wouldn't work as well either, but because I had a better costume than that terrified hitchhiker, I could get picked up even carrying a shotgun! Those were the good old days.

SALT LICK

WHEN YOU'RE ALONE in the backcountry you close your eyes at your own peril. I learned that lesson after I'd worked the whole day on an uncontained forest fire on Little Roundtop Mountain near Metcalf Bottoms. I was really tired. I'd been digging a firebreak for hours, shoveling and raking, and was ready to go home.

Little Roundtop is a mountain that overlooks Wears Valley. It's part of a high ridgeline that forms a natural boundary that runs along the edge of the Park. Little Roundtop is on the northern edge where Blount County, Sevier County, and the National Park all meet.

I was exhausted and ready to leave for the day when my crew boss said, "Can you work a night shift, too?"

I thought to myself, *You've gotta be kidding me.*

He saw the look on my face and said, "All you have to do is hike this new crew in and get them started on patrol, then you can find you a spot off the trail and get some sleep."

Even though I was totally worn out, hungry, and absolutely filthy, I agreed to do it. The money would be good and I could use it.

I met up with my crew of firefighters. They were from Texas. I hiked them up the steep, winding trail and showed them the section where they needed to patrol that night to make sure the fire didn't jump the new fireline.

We'd already made a firebreak, a line on the ground where we'd dug down through the deep leaf litter to the bare dirt so there was nothing there for the fire to burn through. I told the fellows that I was going to patrol another area, but I was really going to look for a soft place to get some sleep.

The air was still full of smoke. It was springtime and the buds were just coming out on the trees, but the leaves weren't out yet, so you could still see in the woods. I found a beautiful ridge top and fluffed me up some leaves for a bed. I used my backpack for a pillow and lay down and soon fell sound asleep.

I don't know how long I'd been sleeping. I didn't even remember going to sleep, but suddenly, just at daybreak, I popped awake and when I opened my eyes, there was something huge looming over me. It was just a shadow and I didn't know what it was. By reflex I threw my hand and feet up in the air and made a startled sound before I was even fully awake.

The dark shape bolted and I got a look at it. It was a deer, an eight-point buck. It had been standing by my feet, sniffing them, probably licking at the salt from my sweat-soaked boots and clothes. When I jerked awake and shouted, the buck went straight up in the air, flipped around, and then ran away at warp speed.

I was relieved and embarrassed at the same time. I was also having an adrenalin rush now, so there was no way I could go back to sleep. It was getting light anyway, so I got up and started the long walk back to where I would meet up with the nighttime crew of firefighters and hike them back to our trucks. After that I had to report to Headquarters for a briefing about my new fire assignment for that day.

You gradually get used to the idea that some animals will approach you looking for salt, especially if your clothes are sweaty. You also learn that if you hold real still and they can't smell you, it's hard for some animals to realize you're a human. Some animals are curious, so if they can't tell what you are, often they'll come over and inspect you. They're normally very shy and scared of people, though, so as soon as they realize you're a person, they take off.

Several years after that deer startled me awake, the wildlife rangers who stayed at Silers Bald were similarly plagued during the night by a bear we nicknamed *Sneaky*. There's a shelter there for hikers, but the rangers who hog hunt stay a short distance away from the shelter, in a tent, because they're carrying a firearm and need a more secure area away from campers.

Sneaky wouldn't confront anybody in an aggressive way, but she'd slip around behind you and grab whatever food she could find or anything with salt on it, like a boot or a towel. She made it hard to sleep. She'd keep sticking her nose into your tent trying to get to a boot.

One of the best hog hunters who worked in the Silers area was Dale Raxter, a true mountain man from North Carolina. Sneaky had once stuck her head into Dale's tent and successfully made off with one of his hiking boots.

After that Dale kept a pile of rocks inside the tent, near his head, and always kept his boots on while sleeping even when using his sleeping bag. This way, not only could he retaliate if Sneaky stuck her head in his tent, but also, with his boots on, he'd be ready to immediately break camp and escape to get away from her if he needed to.

It was a good plan and it worked. But after that Dale became known for having the dirtiest sleeping bag on the mountain.

RUNNING SCARED

I'VE HAD SOME TERRIFYING and embarrassing moments while working alone out in the remote areas of the Park. One of them was in the spring of 1979, when I was working as a backcountry patrol ranger.

A requirement of my job was to hike at least ten miles every day checking on campers, hikers, and fishermen. Over a period of weeks and months, that's a lot of walking. And most of the terrain was new to me. Each day was a different adventure and I loved it. Getting paid to hike and visit with day-hikers and backpackers was a good way to spend time in the mountains.

One afternoon I was on Rough Creek Trail, on my way downhill to Backcountry Campsite #24, Rough Creek. The trail had veered away from the creek so I didn't have the noise of the water rushing over the rocks to drown out the other sounds. It was a quiet and peaceful area.

I was walking along when I heard a high-pitched beeping sound. I'd never heard that kind of sound before, so I was curious about what it was. I stopped and tried to see where it was coming from, but I couldn't locate it.

It didn't stop, so I continued slowly, walking off-trail, to see what the source of the *beep, beep, beep* was. I thought I was getting close to the source and believed it might be coming from under some leaves near the trail. So I bent down, getting closer and closer to the ground, to try to see what it was.

When my head got to within a couple of feet of the ground, suddenly something went off like a rocket, exploding right in my face. An object came hurtling out of the leaf litter and smacked me upside the head. Everything happened so fast, I had no idea what had hit me. For a moment I thought a snake had bitten me.

But whatever it was, it scared the fool out of me, so without thinking I took off, trying to get the heck outta Dodge. I ran down the trail as fast as I could go. I was being chased by something that was repeatedly striking me on top of my head and making an awful squawking noise. I wasn't about to slow down and look back either. After running a few yards, I finally got the nerve to glance over my shoulder to see what the devil was after me.

It was a bird! A bird was flying close behind me, flogging me on the head. It was slashing at me with its talons and it hurt! It wasn't a fearsome eagle or a deadly pterodactyl, though. It was a grouse! A grouse was chasing me, flying right above my head, and striking at me again and again.

Here I was, 6'1" and 225 pounds, running as fast as I could to get away from a pound-and-a-half bird. I gradually slowed down from a run to a walk and when I did, the grouse flew off and immediately started doing a broken wing trick on the side of the trail. She dropped one wing and fluttered around on the ground, pretending to be hurt and helpless.

When she did that I realized it was a mother bird. She was only trying to draw my attention away from her chicks. Her strategy worked. I was in a bit of shock from the unexpected attack, high on adrenalin from the scare, and embarrassed that I'd actually run in terror from a small bird. Without thinking, I picked up a rock intending to go on the attack. Then I realized how silly I was acting and dropped the rock.

After I regained my composure, I continued to hike down the trail, wrestling with my pride. I decided I wouldn't tell anyone that I'd run from a grouse, and I didn't for a long time. Years later, when I finally admitted what I'd done, I learned that this same thing had happened to Pat Patten, a backcountry ranger in North Carolina.

Nature armed that bird with a formidable weapon and technique to protect her chicks. I'd already known better than to mess with Mother Nature, but now I knew not to mess with a mother grouse, either. She was a small package with wings and an attitude. I decided that the next time I heard beeping while walking down a trail, I'd keep going.

HORSING AROUND WITH SATAN

SOMETIMES I NEEDED to take more equipment into the backcountry than I could carry, like hog traps, so on those occasions I rode a horse.

My horse was a good-looking, black as coal fellow named Satan. He was a very high-spirited, edgy, nervous horse that most people were scared of, but I liked him because he was strong enough to carry my gear and my big carcass all day.

The Park Service was able to have a horse as nice as Satan because he was confiscated during a poaching case. In the same way law enforcement officials can confiscate a car, SUV, or truck that people use to get into the Park to poach, they can seize a horse, too.

A good mountain horse is valuable. Not just any horse can work in such rough terrain. It needs skill to walk the rugged paths in the mountains. Satan was fast, sure-footed, and smart at knowing how to safely make his way along the trails without being told. And with his polished gait, he rode smooth and easy, like a big Lincoln Continental.

One night I returned to the Spence Field hog hunting camp after a trip to Russell Field. Before I went to sleep I tethered Satan in some trees downhill from my camp. During the night the weather turned bad. I woke up and realized there was a severe thunderstorm going on. It was windy and pouring rain.

I looked out of my tent to check on Satan and discovered he was lying on his side in the mud! I was horrified. I prayed that he wasn't hurt, but worried that somehow he might've broken a leg.

All I had on was my whitey-tightey underwear, but as fast as I could, I slipped on my boots and hat and jumped out of the tent into the monsoon. I went stomping down the hill through the mud to get a closer look. Satan was lying in an awkward position, kicking violently, with one of his back legs up in the air.

I suspected the lightning and thunder had caused the horse to shy and jump around in fear. Somehow he'd gotten one of his rear legs tangled in a rope and was unable to put his foot down. He must've stood on three legs for as long as he could, but then he'd fallen.

I worked to get the ropes untangled, but it was a dangerous struggle with him kicking all the while. As soon as I managed to get the ropes loose, he jumped back up on his feet. He stood there unrecognizable, totally covered in mud and blowing water from his nose. He wouldn't put any weight on the rear leg that had been entangled in the rope. I hoped there was no nerve damage.

I checked him over as well as I could and he seemed to be alright, except for that rear leg. I fed and watered him again and comforted him as well as I could and he gradually settled down. It was a long wait until dawn to confirm whether he was injured or not, but at least the rain had washed most of the mud off the big guy by morning.

It was a bad night, a scary night, waiting for daylight. But, lucky for Satan, everything turned out fine. We loaded up the next morning and started the six mile trip back to the barn in Cades Cove. Because of his sore leg, I didn't think he should have to carry me, so I walked the whole way.

Satan was a very intelligent horse, and I thought a lot of him, so I gave him the benefit of the doubt and assumed that he wasn't faking an injury. If he did, he was a good actor.

The next time I went out riding Satan, Buck went with me. This was the first time Buck had gone anywhere with me since the fiasco when he attempted to teach me how to hunt wild hogs.

It was on a weekend and the plan was to haul supplies and gear down the Appalachian Trail and end up at Gregory Bald. The hog hunters' camps along the Appalachian Trail each have a fifty-five gallon metal barrel that would seal and lock. The drums were used to cache spare clothes for the government hog hunters and the corn to bait hog traps. If we hauled in supplies and gear by horseback, the rangers wouldn't have to carry in as much on foot and could use more of their energy to look for pesky creatures.

We started at Clingmans Dome. It was a long day, nine miles to Derrick Knob, and over twenty-five miles round trip. It got dark when we were on the way back. That's when the trouble started.

Buck always rode the same horse, *Ole Granny*. She was a small, temperamental horse with a love of peanut butter and jelly and she got along well with Buck. When Buck rode at night he had a policy of never turning on a flashlight because it would ruin your night vision—and more importantly, it would ruin your horse's night vision. But it worried me to ride in the dark.

It was *really* dark where we were. It was a cloudy night and we were riding in dense woods. I couldn't see *anything* and I just couldn't stand it, so every once in a while I'd flip my light on very briefly. This upset Buck, of course. "Boy," he said, "the only time ye need to turn a light on is if ye cain't hear yer horse's hoofs. If ye cain't hear yer horse's hoofs hittin rocks, ye kin turn on a light to see if he's walked off the bluff."

Wouldn't that be too late?, I wondered, but I was afraid to question any aspects of the limited amount of training he was willing to give me. I'd ridden and worked horses and mules on the farm, but it had been nothing like this. What we were doing seemed crazy to me. Why couldn't we use flashlights all the time? We had plenty of batteries.

Despite trying hard to do what he said, I couldn't resist flicking my light on a few more times when I became unable to tolerate riding along the dangerous narrow trails in the dark. Whenever I turned my light on, Buck would wheel around and look at me with a big chew of tobacco bulging in his cheek. I could tell it annoyed him, but he didn't say anything. He was a man of few words, and he'd given up trying to make a real mountain man out of me.

I was on my own.

One of my strangest night rides happened during the mid-1980s when I was alone and taking Buck's advice about not using my flashlight. The wildlife crew who would normally have been in the backcountry were attending law enforcement training, so I told them to go ahead and bait their traps and promised to ride up and check on them.

It made for a long day by the time I finally got all the traps checked along the Appalachian Trail between Thunderhead Mountain and Buckeye Gap. As I rode down the mountain, it got dark. I was riding Satan down a trail above Tremont, on the Lynn Camp Prong Trail. We came around a curve onto a straight section of the trail where, if it had been daylight, you'd have been able to see a couple of hundred yards ahead.

Suddenly, without any warning, thousands of fireflies blinked on at the same time. Their simultaneous blinking lit up a long stretch of trail in front of me like landing lights on an airport runway. It was amazing. Then, just as suddenly as they'd lit up, they all blinked off together and left me and Satan with night blindness.

It was the weirdest thing I'd ever seen. I couldn't understand what I'd just witnessed. Satan was disturbed by it, too. Then it happened again, the fireflies lit up at the same time and after a few seconds they all went dark at the same time. They did it over and over and Satan spooked each time they lit up.

I had no idea what was going on and wondered, *How are they doing that? How could they possibly being doing that?* It was unbelievable.

We continued along the trail, with Satan jerking and shying from the synchronized blinking. Each time the fireflies lit up, you could see all the way along the trail, then they'd go dark and you couldn't see anything at all.

Although I was blinded by the insects' flashing, I could feel Satan tossing his head and hear his bridle and bit jingling and rattling as he moved. I had to trust Satan to find his way along the trail and he did. We got home safely.

Now, of course, I know what we were seeing that night. It's a rare type of synchronous firefly that lives in a few places around the world. Scientists from Tennessee used to travel to Asia to study them until they realized we had them right here! Nowadays in June, tens of thousands of people come from all over the world to see the show.

That first time was spooky, though. It was yet another of the unexpected things that raised my blood pressure when I was out in the backcountry alone, and this time it turned out I'd been terrorized by lightning bugs! It's kind of cool to see them now, doing their thing, but that first time Satan and I saw them, I thought I had wandered into an episode of *The Twilight Zone.*

RUNNING FOR HOME

THE WEATHER IN THE SMOKIES can be as dangerous as the terrain or the animals. Some of the scariest and closest calls I had were with the elements.

Up in the higher altitudes of the Park you have to beware of hypo- or hyperthermia, wind, lightning, or falling trees. The higher areas also have reduced air quality because of environmental pollution and this can become an issue when you're breathing heavily, especially if you have any medical problems. In the lower elevations, you have to watch out for flash flooding and landslides caused by heavy rains.

The mountains send down enormous amounts of water after a heavy or prolonged rain. The water concentrates in the creases of the watersheds and thunders downhill carrying entire trees or even whole sections of the forest with it. This *power-washing* of the ground wears the mountains down and rounds off the sharp edges, making them look deceptively gentle. But the Smokies are neither gentle nor forgiving, they're just very, very old.

One early summer night when I was hog hunting in the back-country near Gregory Bald, I began to hear rumbling. As I walked along it got louder and I saw lightning in the distance, so I knew it was a thunderstorm. I used my radio to call Dispatch and find out where the storm was and which way it was moving.

When I saw a lightning flash, I'd count off the seconds until I heard the thunder to try to estimate how far away the danger was. It worried me a little because it seemed like the storm might be heading toward me from the west.

I was trying to figure out how long it would take the bad weather to reach me because I wanted to spend as much time as I could searching for hogs during the prime hunting hours which were from dusk to around 11 p.m. A bad electrical storm would present a real problem, though, because I had no real protection. I decided to pick up the pace. Even then, I could see the lightning was getting brighter and the thunder was getting louder.

Within minutes I realized I wasn't going to make it back to camp before the storm hit, so I broke into a run. I was sweating and breathing hard from exertion, running along a narrow, open, high-elevation trail that was deeply rutted in the center from being pounded by thousands of boots and hooves and from years of torrential water runoff.

There's a great deal of moisture in the Smokies when you're near 5,000' elevation. Some years this part of the Park got seven or even eight feet of rain and qualified as a temperate rainforest. I ran through the Appalachian jungle as fast as I could, but before long, the storm caught up with me.

Even though it was pouring rain, I didn't bother to stop and put on my rain suit because I was sweating so much from exertion. My waterproof suit wasn't breathable, so it would be hot and uncomfortable. I'd be just as miserable wearing it as I would without it, so I decided not to fool with it. That meant my only protection from the elements was my Park Service baseball cap and short-sleeve cotton uniform and pants.

My feet were soon soaked and blistered. I was tearing them up running the trail in wet socks and boots. I couldn't see the ground because of the long grass and because there was so much water running down the center of the trail. My boots were underwater. That's really hard on boots. One sole had already come unglued and was flopping and popping as I ran down the trail. I could feel the other one loosening.

The ground was supersaturated, so I was fully grounded if lightning struck. Suddenly I stumbled and hit the ground like a big bull crashing into a wall. Hard falls like that were nearly guaranteed if you're running around in the wilderness in the dark.

I'd camped at Moore Springs because there was good drinking water there. When I started running, I was two miles away from my camp, working my way toward Parsons Branch. That meant I had to cross the wide open spaces on Gregory Bald to get back to my tent.

I was running as fast as I could go carrying a daypack and a shotgun along a path that was just a muddy stream. It was especially dark on account of the heavy clouds and rain. I still had a ways to go when the lightning got to where I was. It caught me right out in the open as I was crossing Gregory Bald. Lightning was hitting in the field all around me, striking the trees and the ground.

Even on a bright, sunny day the balds are strange places. They're extraordinary because they have the best views and can be the most beautiful places in the Park, especially when the azaleas are in bloom. But nobody really understands why they exhibit a totally different type of plant life than the rest of the Park. At night, in the midst of a violent storm, the great open stretch lit up with bolts of lightning and was downright terrifying.

I danced all the way across the bald, stumbling and falling over holes and rocks, hoping and praying that I wouldn't get struck by lightning. The fact that I was carrying a shotgun across the top of a ridge in an electrical storm didn't help. That wasn't smart. I wanted to throw the gun down, but at the same time I didn't want to ruin it or abandon my only means of dealing with a group of wild hogs. I thought sure I'd be hit by lightning.

I'd stumble and fall and then lie face down on the wet ground for a few seconds trying to catch my breath. Then the lightning would hit near me and I'd jump up and take off running again. Each time it thundered, I flinched. I was soaked and muddy and out of breath, right on the edge of being in a total panic.

I fell several times going across the bald but didn't dare risk staying on the ground, out in the open, for very long. The crashing and sizzling of the lightning strikes nearby kept motivating me to get back up and run. I didn't know if I was better off lying flat on the ground or standing up. There was nowhere that seemed safe.

I didn't know what else to do, so I kept running and running. It didn't make sense, because my camp wasn't going to be a lot safer. How much could a nylon tent help? I'd be out of the rain, but there were a lot of trees there. I guess people just have a natural instinct when they're scared to try to get *home*, no matter what form that might take. That night, my tent at Moore Springs was home.

So I kept going, trying to get back to my camp, intending to take off my wet, muddy clothes and hang them out in the torrential downpour on a parachute cord. That way they'd get a good old-fashioned washing.

But when I finally made it back to camp, I was so exhausted and miserable I just wadded up my clothes and threw myself into my tent. I crawled into my sleeping bag and lay there, awake, for most of the night. I didn't get a lot of sleep because you can't sleep when the weather is like that.

I rarely got a good night's sleep in the backcountry on account of the weather and the wild animals. There was *always* something going on. Even in good weather, you hear a lot more than just the crickets when you're lying out there in the dark.

The high winds are dangerous and unpredictable, too. During windstorms I'd lie in my tent and listen to big trees falling, popping and cracking, then crashing as they went down. When the big ones hit the ground, it sure got your attention.

But you never know where to go to be safe. There was no guaranteed safe place. So I prayed a lot. That night during the storm on Gregory Bald and countless other nights in my three decades in the Park, all I could do before I went to sleep was hope and pray I wasn't going to be at the wrong place at the wrong time.

IN A FLASH

I HIKED INTO THE BACKCOUNTRY and camped for a week in the early 1980s. It was May and I was working the area between Double Springs Shelter and Silers Bald Shelter, looking for wild hogs.

I went up on Monday and came out on Friday. On alternate nights, I slept in the Silers Bald or Double Springs Shelters. This was back when the shelters had bunks framed with logs and bottoms made of welded wire mesh, like the wire used to make small animal cages. The wire beds had become concave, sagging from the weight of so many people sitting and sleeping on them over the years, so it was kind of like sleeping in the bottom of a boat or in a hammock.

On Friday I was walking out of the backcountry, travelling west on the Appalachian Trail, hiking toward Buckeye Gap, then down Miry Ridge, planning to come out at Elkmont at Jakes Creek.

On my way out, I encountered a young couple who were hiking east. Rangers always try to speak to everyone we pass on the trail, especially in the backcountry, to make sure they're doing okay, educate them about our hog hunting activities, ask them if they've encountered any bears, and answer any questions they might have.

I'd been alone all week except for crossing paths with a few solo backpackers, so I was happy to see and talk to other people. I stopped and chatted with the couple. They were having a great time. They said they were planning to spend the night in the Double Springs Shelter. We chatted about the trail and their route and the weather, then I said goodbye and hiked on out.

The next morning I heard that someone had been killed the previous evening at the Double Springs Shelter. It was the young man. He and the young woman were inside the shelter during a thunderstorm, sitting on a wire mesh bunk. They were sitting side by side, but the girl was seated on an Ensolite sleeping pad, so she had some insulation between her and the wire.

Apparently lightning struck the ground near the shelter and ran along an underground tree root to the foundation of the building. It continued to the wire mesh bunk and electrocuted the young fellow.

He was just in his twenties.

I couldn't get over it. I'd spent the night in the same shelter many times and slept on wire beds in many other shelters. And I'd travelled along the ridges during thunderstorms many times. It really shook me up.

It makes you see how fragile life is. The Park is beautiful, but nature can turn deadly without much warning. And sometimes you don't get a second chance.

RACCOON!

WE PUT A LOT OF EFFORT into keeping bears away from people and from human food. This is the fundamental way to protect wild black bears and it's the very best thing we can do to make sure the bears have good lives and are able to live out their full lifespan in relative peace and good health in the wild.

We try to educate people about how to handle their food inside the Park, and we provide bear-proof dumpsters so they can dispose of their garbage properly. We've modified the design of these dumpsters over the years to make them easy for humans to open and close, but impossible for most bears to manage—most, but not *all*, bears.

Once upon a time there was a small adult female bear, Bear #287, who learned to open the latch on the dumpsters at Cades Cove picnic area. Unfortunately, after she got it open, she fell in and the lid slammed shut and latched, trapping her inside the dumpster. While she rummaged around in the garbage and ate scraps from people's picnics, a trash truck came along and picked up the dumpster and emptied it into the back of the trash truck—bear and all.

Because of the way the dumpster was emptied on big hooks high over the top of the truck, the trash men didn't see they'd just dumped a live bear into the truck along with the load of trash. So they compacted the trash as usual, which should've spelled doom for the trapped bear. The garbage collectors made a few more stops inside the Park and emptied the rest of the dumpsters, compacting the trash they collected each time. Then they took their load to the waste recycling center in Sevierville.

The driver of the trash truck still had no idea there was a bear in the back of his truck, so he dumped his load of trash as usual and left. The men who worked at the recycling center approached the fresh pile of trash to sort out the things that could be recycled. As they were picking through the material, suddenly, a very frightened small bear popped up out of the garbage.

The animal was injured and in pain from being compacted several times. She was scared to death after all the experiences she'd undergone that day, so she bluff-charged the men. The fellows had no previous experience with bears, so they ran off, trying to put as much space as possible between them and the bear. The men and the bear ran into a nearby building at the recycling center where the terrified cub climbed a metal I-beam as high as she could go, trying to find a safe place.

None of the workers who'd seen the bear spoke English as their first language. The closest word any of them knew to describe the animal was *raccoon*. So they ran to their boss shouting, "Raccoon! Raccoon!!"

The boss thought the group of grown men was seriously overreacting to having seen a raccoon. So, he didn't pay much attention to them at first. After a few more minutes of hysterical shouting and gesturing the men finally convinced their boss to come take a look. They took him into the building and pointed up at the bear in the rafters.

Oh, the boss thought, *raccoon! That's not a raccoon, that's a dang bear!* Now he understood what all the hoopla was about.

The boss quickly made some phone calls. The Tennessee Wildlife Resources Agency and the National Park Service came to the recycling center where they darted the terrified animal. Unfortunately, she went to sleep up in the rafters, draped across a metal I-beam. This meant the rangers had to go get a bucket truck and use a boom to retrieve the sleeping bear and lower her to the ground.

We were concerned that the small bear seemed to have some internal injuries from being compacted, so she was taken to the University of Tennessee College of Veterinary Medicine where she was evaluated. After she had x-rays, blood work, and multiple examinations, it was determined that she had a ruptured urinary tract. She was given strong antibiotics and fluids to give her a chance to heal, but her prognosis wasn't very good.

Rather than putting her down, though, we decided to let her tell us if she could make it or not. We transferred her to the Wildlife Building where we fed and watered her and kept a close eye on her condition. If she'd appeared to be in constant pain, we thought it would be best to put her down, but we knew wild animals were unbelievably resilient, so we wanted to give her a chance to recover.

A few days after her terrible ordeal in the trash truck, we came in one morning and found her trying to climb the chain link fence enclosure she was in. Obviously she was feeling better!

Within a couple of weeks, the small bear was strong enough to be released back into the wild. We took her to Mt. Sterling on the east end of the Park. As the crow flies, that was about thirty-five miles from Cades Cove. We moved her as far as possible in the Park hoping she would break her dependence on garbage.

About a year later we got a call from a Cades Cove ranger saying a mother bear and a cub were trying to get trash from the garbage cans in the picnic area. We captured them and realized we had the bear who'd ridden in the trash truck. But this time she wasn't alone. She had a cub that she was now teaching to be a garbage bear.

We moved the two bears to a remote area of the Cherokee National Forest and gave the mother bear another chance to live. Years passed and we never heard of Bear #287 again. So we hope that she'd learned to run not only from the sight of a garbage truck, but also to run from the sight of garbage cans.

APPALACHIAN BEAR RESCUE

I'VE HAD TO EUTHANIZE perfectly healthy little bear cubs when they were orphaned, for example, because the mother was killed by poachers or a car, or maybe a cub was abandoned and became separated from its family. In those days, there was no legitimate place to raise them and keep them wild so they could be released back into the wild. If we simply released them, they would die of starvation of be killed and eaten by other animals.

Putting them down was terrible and one of the toughest things I ever had to do while at the Park. I just couldn't stand to put any more little cubs down. There had to be a better way.

In the late 1980s there was a major covert operation, called *Operation Smoky*, that exposed a significant amount of illegal trade in bear parts, mainly selling gallbladders. News about the poaching was upsetting to the public. Many people came out of the woodwork wanting to do something, anything, to help bears. One lady from Atlanta wanted to buy machine guns for Park rangers to use to shoot poachers.

In a conversation with this lady, I tried to educate her about bear management and the real needs we had. Once she heard that little orphaned cubs were being put down, she asked how she could help. I explained to her that we needed to get a place set up where we could take orphaned, starving, sick, or injured wild black bears.

To help protect the wild behavior of the animals, people had to be restricted from interacting with them. We needed a place where they could be taken care of for a short time, then as quickly as possible transitioned back into the wild.

We wouldn't keep bears forever, but we could help them get over the hump and save a lot of young injured or orphaned bears. So over the years and with the help of a lot of good people a facility was developed that came to be known as Appalachian Bear Rescue, or

ABR.

The Park is a tough place to live, even for wild animals. So when we see an animal having a problem, we try to help it out if possible. For example, one morning some people noticed a small bear limping around behind the Park Headquarters building.

We investigated and discovered it was a yearling bear with broken hind leg. Because of its limp, the bear was nicknamed *Chester* after a character on *Gunsmoke*. The malnourished little bear weighed only about thirty pounds. That's small for a recently weaned yearling bear. We didn't know how Chester got hurt, but we suspect he was accidentally injured by his mother when she was trying to wean him.

We captured Chester and took him to the University of Tennessee Veterinary Hospital where they put a plate in to repair his broken femur. Then we took him to Appalachian Bear Rescue where he was kept for nearly a year. He actually hibernated there over the winter.

In the spring when he woke up, Chester had to go back to the vet school for a follow-up surgery to his leg. Luckily everything went well, so after a short stint back at ABR we released him just above Park Headquarters near where we'd first seen him. The limping thirty pound yearling was now a healthy 150 pound adult bear ready to go back into the wild.

A month or two following the release, I got a call from Deener Matthews, innkeeper and owner of a world famous bed and breakfast inn called *The Swag* located along the Park boundary between Cataloochee and Maggie Valley, North Carolina. Deener was seeing a bear eating apples from her tree. It had an ear tag. She gave us the number and we identified it as Chester.

Rick Varner went over to capture Chester and confirm that his leg had healed properly. We also wanted Rick to move Chester away from The Swag. We didn't want the bear hanging around that close to people. We hoped the capture would be a negative experience associated with that particular area and he'd stay away in wilder territory.

Even though we'd released Chester back into his home territory in the Park Headquarters area, he travelled on his own in excess of thirty miles as the crow flies, on rough ground through the mountains. So clearly his leg was healed.

After Rick released Chester, there were no further reports of him, so we hope everything continued to go well. We believed it was a happy ending to the story. If we didn't have Appalachian Bear Rescue, Chester wouldn't have gotten a second chance. But because of many caring people, he did.

ANYONE WHO WORKS AROUND BEARS can tell you— **People who feed bears, kill bears. Period.**

The biggest problem wildlife rangers face in dealing with black bears is that people feed them. Human food is an enormous threat to wildlife in the Great Smoky Mountains National Park. Visitors have been told for fifty years that *Garbage Kills Bears* and *A Fed Bear is a Dead Bear*, but somehow it doesn't sink in. For various stupid reasons, some people won't stop feeding the bears.

Bears who eat garbage don't eat just eat the food in the garbage, but they chew up whatever inedible material is in it as well. It is quite common when a garbage bear is trapped, to see that its fecal matter includes aluminum foil and plastic wrappers.

Human food is also hard on a bear's teeth. It can rot them or they may get broken chewing garbage. Bad teeth make it very difficult for the bear to survive. People don't remember this nowadays, but before humans gained widespread access to dental care, one of the leading causes of death was from tooth problems.

Wild bears don't have reliable access to dental care, so problems with their teeth have devastating consequences for them. Rotted, broken, or missing teeth significantly impair their ability to adequately feed and survive. If you can't eat, you won't live.

To help Appalachian Bear Rescue get started, the wildlife crew donated labor and we built the fences using whatever scraps and leftovers we could find. We repaired and donated old broken bear and hog cages and traps, so there'd be a way to move the cubs to and from the Park, ABR, and the vet hospital. This provided a safe way to handle the cubs while they were being cared for.

The cub compound is surrounded by a tall chain link fence, with a wide alley just inside it. Then there's another tall chain link fence covered with a thick black Geotech fabric to obscure the bear's view of the people who provide their food. This inner chain link fence is also fortified with several strands of electrified high-tensile wire.

Wild animals hate electricity. An electric fence is more of a mental barrier than a physical one, but they work. No bear has ever escaped the confines of ABR.

There's a huge amount of labor involved in feeding and caring for bears and its done 24/7 by a tiny, dedicated staff. Appalachian Bear Rescue has helped nearly 200 bears so far and only one of the animals following release from the facility has ever been reported as a *garbage* or *nuisance* bear. That's an impressive record, especially since some of the bears they receive have already had some contact with humans.

ABR attributes this record to the strict procedures established by the Tennessee Wildlife Resources Agency, which is responsible for overseeing the facility. ABR can't display black bears. Other than a zoo, no facility is allowed to do that because it would create a demand for illegally captured wild bears.

A cub is accepted at ABR only when it's known to have been orphaned for a certain amount of time, to give the mother the chance to return, if she's still alive. If the mother doesn't return, the cub can be captured by wildlife officials and brought to ABR.

ABR has received malnourished bears and bears with a variety of ailments and injuries such as broken legs, serious lacerations, infections, neurological problems, or loss of an eye. One of the most common types of bears they receive is orphaned cubs.

Cubs left unattended in the wild won't live long. They'll die of starvation or be killed by a coyote, bobcat, dog, or even another bear. Their chances of survival would be zero.

If the cub is young and weighs only a few pounds, it's immediately placed on a commercial formula and bowl or bottle fed every three to four hours. It's normally housed with other cubs for comfort and companionship. If the cub is a newborn, wildlife officials immediately begin the search for a suitable surrogate mother in the wild while the cub receives interim care at ABR.

There are usually ongoing bear research projects where mother bears are wearing radio-collars so the researchers can locate them in their winter dens and check on their overall condition and see if they have any newborn cubs.

Ideally a cub will be kept wild by being introduced to a surrogate mother and siblings very quickly. If that's not possible, the cub is raised at ABR with minimal human interaction and later released back into the wild.

Other injured, sick, or malnourished bears arriving at ABR are, depending on their condition, placed in a one-acre bear enclosure which has hardwood trees, natural dens, and man-made streams and pools. Some may need veterinary care before they're released into the larger enclosure. Once they're put inside the bear enclosure, the cubs rarely see humans or receive human contact unless they need medical attention. This is their last stop before being released back into the wild.

During feeding times the keeper tosses food over the eight-foot-tall covered fence and scatters it so the cubs have to forage to find it. The bears' diet consists of fruits, berries, nuts, and some vegetables that are similar to the natural diet they'll find in their normal habitat. Guidelines from TWRA state that bears must weigh at least fifty pounds before they can sustain themselves in the wild.

ABR makes sure the bears are an acceptable weight and in good health, and that they exhibit normal foraging behavior and interact and vocalize with other bears. The little bears must also have climbing skills. They should exhibit positive bear behavior by staying up in trees during the day and coming down at night to eat. If they are moving around for short periods during the day, they should immediately retreat to the trees when they hear unusual noises or smell unusual odors. This is normal behavior for survival in the wild.

The goal at ABR is to make sure the bears don't associate with people on any level. During their months in residence without any human contact, the bears are naturally cautious and afraid of people and will retreat to the trees for safety if they hear humans or strange sounds. This is one of the reasons why TWRA doesn't allow visitors.

When all the criteria are met, bears are prepared for release back into the wild. Bears from the Great Smoky Mountains National Park will be returned to a place close to where they were found. Cubs admitted from Tennessee but outside the national park, will be released in one of the TWRA's wildlife management areas or bear sanctuaries that offer thousands of acres of plentiful food, water, and a safe habitat. Bears admitted from out-of-state wildlife agencies will be returned to their home states.

When they're ready for release, bears are trapped and put into small holding areas. They're injected with a sedative when officials arrive to transport them. This gives workers approximately an hour to perform a final health check and to measure and weigh them. During this final exam, if the animals are large enough, they're given numbered ear tags and lip tattoos for identification purposes. Because the bears are sedated they're not aware of any of these procedures. Then they're loaded into a special cage for transport.

ABR tries to release the cubs in pairs, though there's no scientific data to support the idea that the cubs stay together in the wild. Bears tend to be solitary animals, except during breeding season or in areas where food sources are concentrated and abundant. Though they may have had interactions with other bears while at ABR, their natural instincts will tell them to make their way in the wild alone.

One exception to the hands-off procedure is when an injured cub or yearling is admitted to ABR. In that situation, the injured bear is typically treated at the University of Tennessee Veterinary Hospital and allowed to recuperate at ABR. Then the hands-off procedures are reinstated. There's normally no time limit for recuperation of an injured animal. Every case is different.

The injured bear is given all the time it needs in order to heal and rehabilitate from its injury. From time to time the recuperation period requires that the injured bear has to be kept all winter at ABR. When this occurs, the bear hibernates at the facility and is released the following spring or summer after it has fully recovered.

ABR has given nearly 200 injured or sick baby bears, cubs and yearlings a second chance to live. I know if bears could talk, they'd say, *Thanks ABR, you saved my life.*

BEAST ON A LEASH

MOST OF OUR INSIGHT into handling large wild animals like bears and boars has been learned by trial and error. Some days it was mostly error, like the day I grabbed hold of a wild boar and then realized I had no idea what to do next.

I was working with two locally notorious characters, Jerry and Larry, two mountain men who worked for the Tennessee Wildlife Resources Agency as wildlife technicians in the Tellico area.

We had a seventy-pound wild hog in the main room of the Wildlife Building in a twelve-by-fourteen-foot animal holding cage made of chain link fence. We were holding the pig until the TWRA could come get it and take it to the Tellico Wildlife Management Area for release.

Jerry and Larry were a lot of fun to work with. Larry was a thinker. Jerry was more of a talker. Jerry was tall and slender and particularly memorable for his tendency to wear a mismatched plaid shirt and plaid pants at the same time.

Jerry was shy and didn't like to look anyone in the eye. He was also fidgety and talked fast, but he was always the first one to jump in and help. He was an extremely hard-working, dedicated, and competent guy. Whenever we met to transfer a wild hog or black bear from the Park to a TWRA management area, he'd be wringing his hands and patting his foot, wanting to get going.

If I ever had to pick a person to help me handle large wild animals, it'd be Jerry. He'd handled more wild hogs, black bears, and deer than I'd probably even seen. He's a good friend and a true professional.

On this particular day, Jerry came to pick up the captured wild hog and we went into the large room in the Wildlife Building where the pig was being held in a cage. "Pull him out here," Jerry said, pointing at the hog, "and we'll shoot the medicine to him."

Medicine was how Jerry referred to the tranquilizer drugs we used to calm animals that were being transported. "How am I gonna pull him out?" I asked.

"I don't know," Jerry said, with a smile, "that's your job."

While I rummaged around in our equipment for a catch pole, Jerry got the drug kit. This catch pole was an extendable four-to-six-foot extendable aluminum pole with a loop on one end that's made of plastic-coated cable. The cable can be tightened or loosened as needed to snag a critter. It's basically a small lasso on a long stick.

When we were ready to move the beast to Jerry's transfer box, I opened the cage door and the hog instantly came exploding toward us at top speed, huffing, slobbering, and blowing snot and other wild hog nasal secretions all over Jerry and me.

I managed to lasso it, but the cable caught around the hog's snout instead of its neck. The critter immediately started squealing, jumping up and down, and carrying on like I was trying to kill it or it kill me.

All I wanted to do was ship the hog to Tellico where it would be turned loose and could run wild and free again. I didn't want to hurt it, but I don't think the hog felt the same about me or Jerry.

"I'm gonna pull it up to the cage door," I shouted, "and you give it the shot. Be quick, I'm not sure how long I can hold it!"

"Yeah, yeah, yeah, we'll do that," Jerry agreed.

I pulled the hog toward me, but when I got it to the edge of the cage, at the opening of the door, neither Jerry nor I could stop it. It kept going and bolted right out of the cage, into the big room.

The hog ran full throttle around the room, through buckets, feed sacks, drug kits, shovels, rakes, axes—everything we kept stored in there. I had a hold on it with the pole, but I couldn't get any leverage to stop it from running, so it galloped in a circle spinning me around and around like a top as it went.

"Jerry," I hollered, as the hog zoomed around the room, "get outta the way!"

Jerry had to jump the catch pole every time the pig circled the room. We couldn't keep this up for long. I was getting extremely dizzy and tired and Jerry wasn't young enough to keep leaping the pole forever. The room was in a shambles.

"Catch it!" I hollered.

"I can't!" Jerry shouted back.

Then we'd repeat our shouting on the hog's next lap.

"Catch it!"

"I can't!"

Eventually I was able to maneuver the hog into a corner of the room so Jerry could jump on it and give it the shot of immobilization drugs to settle it down. When the beast was finally back under control, both of us were totally out of breath from all the spinning, leaping, and shouting, and we were both laughing.

I looked around the room and it literally looked like a tornado had passed through. Nothing was where it was supposed to be except the hog.

"You shoulda seen yourself goin around and around," Jerry said, "You looked like an upside down helicopter!"

"Well," I said, "you looked like a little girl jumping rope!"

Soon Jerry took the pig off to its new home, leaving me to clean up the mess.

DUMB LUCK

THANK GOODNESS I inherited a particular kind of dumb luck from my Dad. I think we may have some help from above as well. We both have an uncanny ability to survive chaotic episodes with animals and vehicles. We routinely get into trouble, but, so far, we've always managed to live through it.

I've learned from watching my Dad all my life that you can't accidentally kill yourself until the Lord says it's your time to go. Dad's had countless accidental brushes with death, but he always seems to pull through.

He fell off a twenty-eight foot silo, twice. Once he fell to the inside when he was climbing a ladder and the top step broke, and the other time he fell to the outside into a muddy barnyard. He was lying on his back in mud and cow manure, mainly cow manure, when his helper found him and said, "Bill, Bill are you okay? How far you'd fall?"

"All the way to the ground," Dad said.

He's wrecked three different tractors by trying to drive them on extremely steep hills on our farm. These are 45% slopes, rutted with cow paths. For anyone with an instinct for self-preservation, they're *way* too steep to be running a tractor on, but, of course, Dad doesn't have any sense of self-preservation. He turned one tractor over on himself when he was eighty years old and was saved only by the rollbar.

Another one he turned over sideways, was thrown clear, and watched it roll to the bottom of the hill. The third one I was on with him! We were off-loading tobacco stalks on a frosty early morning when the tractor started sliding. Dad and I jumped off onto the uphill side and the tractor and trailer rolled off of a bluff and crashed into a tree.

He's turned two ATVs over on himself, at least that's all he's admitted to anyone. One of them he careened into a ditch and turned over on top of himself right after he'd had bypass surgery.

A cow once kicked him in the head and cracked his skull. At various times he's gotten a mouth full, a nose full, an eye full, and an ear full of 100-proof cow poop. It never seemed to faze him in the least.

Working on the farm, spraying for insects, weeds, brush, tobacco, and animal parasites, he's licked, wiped, rubbed, absorbed, or ingested nearly every dangerous chemical known to man, but he just keeps going.

Dad was a rural mail carrier for forty years. They don't watch the road—at least he didn't. He was always looking at the mail or the mailbox, but not so much at the road. He drives a tractor or an ATV the same way. Instead of looking where he's going, he looks at cows or a cornfield, or a John Deere tractor sitting along the road, while he drives off into the unknown.

He fell off the roof of the house once when he was adjusting the antenna. Momma said she came home from work and found him lying in the yard, playing with our dachshund, Hotdog. She didn't realize he was hurt, but he was. He'd broken some ribs and couldn't get up without her help.

He probably takes too much medicine, as many older people do. Some of them make him dizzy and unstable on his feet. If you didn't know that my Dad has never had a drink of alcohol in his life, you might assume by the way he walks that he just returned from a seven-day drunk.

Once he was climbing off a tractor that was parked on a bridge and walked right off it and fell ten feet into the creek below. Thank heavens there was enough water in the creek to help break his fall. He got up, climbed back up the bank and got right back on the tractor like nothing had ever happened.

He's been thrown off mules, bitten by dogs, run over by charging bulls, fallen off fences, mashed the heebie-jeebies out of his fingers, and fallen into every hole east of the Mississippi. Mom always said, "Son, your Dad is gonna kill himself someday, but he'll die doing what he loves."

I'm not really sure that's true, though. The way I see it is that my Dad has, with all his antics and escapades, nearly killed himself over and over, but he always manages to survive. I've learned from watching my Dad that no matter what you do, you ain't gonna go until the Lord says it's your time to go.

So I have that heritage, genes, and training—a tendency to have a lot of dumb accidents, offset by enough dumb luck to survive them. All I can say is, *Thank you Dear God up above.*

SKY DIVING CUB

SOME POACHING GOES ON in the Park and always will. We believe it's less than it used to be. We hope so anyway, for several reasons.

Not only do poachers kill big male bears, but sometimes they kill the mother bear and leave her orphaned cubs behind. Often her cubs aren't old enough to survive on their own, so unless we do something, they'll die from starvation or be killed by other bears.

It was early one morning when I got a call about a very small bear seen up in a tree at the upper end of the Chimneys picnic area, about five miles up the mountain from Headquarters. When we got there we found the little cub near the top of a large Silverbell tree. As soon as we got out of our vehicle, we could hear it crying for his mom. He was scared and hungry.

There was a large pool of blood at the base of the tree, so we assumed that poachers had shot and killed the mother bear during the night and had taken her body away and left the little orphaned cub hiding up in the tree where his mother had sent him for safety when the poachers approached her. It was a sad sight. Everyone pleaded for us to do something. The cub's cries were heart-wrenching.

I looked up the tree and realized it was a long way to the cub. I had a ladder that would reach about sixteen feet. Then I could use portable climbing steps by hanging them onto tree branches to climb even higher. I also had a catch pole I could use to reach another ten feet or so.

The orphaned cub was young. He weighed only about ten or twelve pounds. No doubt he was scared as well as hungry. His mom was gone forever. But just because he was small, don't think he couldn't do a *lot* of damage to a person.

A little bear is like a wildcat on steroids. I wasn't looking forward to tangling with him. When it comes to grabbing hold of a bear cub, size doesn't matter!

By the time I arrived at the picnic area, there was already a crowd of about 150 people gathered to watch. There were a bunch of cameras out, too, both still and video. There was even a national news crew there for some reason. Whatever happened, good or bad, it was obvious the episode would be captured and replayed many times.

I worried about how the capture attempt would turn out—I could look like a hero, I could get humiliated, or I could fall out of the tree and die. I was hoping for the first option.

One of the onlookers had nicknamed the cub Les, after Les Nessman from the show *WKRP in Cincinnati*. I normally frown on naming wild animals in the Park, but the name was catchy and suited the little bear.

When I got to the tree, I really didn't have a definite plan because I didn't know what the cub would do when I approached him. Would he climb down and scratch and bite me in the face? Would he scamper up to the top of the tree? Would he leap to his death in front of a crowd of concerned onlookers as soon as I got near him?

I had no idea how he'd react. All I could do was climb the tree, hope for the best, and maybe I'd be able to capture the cub and get back on the ground with both of us in one piece. But, just in case my strategy didn't go as planned, we set up a catch net at the base of the tree, held by rangers and a couple of the visitors. The catch net was made of nylon shark netting we used to make wild hogs traps.

I said a quick prayer, positioned the ladder, picked up the climbing steps and catch pole, and took a deep breath. I climbed as high as I could, first on the long ladder, then on the hanging steps, then on small limbs, holding onto the trunk of the tree for dear life.

I didn't dare go any higher. Safety-wise, I was already too high. If our Park safety officer had seen me up in that tree, he'd have had a heart attack on the spot. The cub and I were both clinging to the main trunk, but it was only about six inches in diameter. The tree was swaying with my 235 pounds of bodyweight. I heard the clicking of many shutters and glanced down to see dozens of cameras pointed up at me and Les.

I slid the catch pole up the side of the tree, thinking I could put it around the bear's body, tighten it up, then lower him with the pole, and release him into the net. Things didn't go as well as I'd hoped. The instant I touched the cub with the little loop of rope on the end of the catch pole he bolted down the tree, butt first, like a runaway elevator.

As the descending cub got closer, I quickly realized there wasn't enough room for him to pass me on the narrow trunk. The cub came level with my face and started woofing at me from the other side of the little tree trunk. His upper lip was extended and he was blowing and making rapid popping sounds with his jaws.

I was holding onto the tree with one arm and leaning away from the trunk, getting my head back as far as possible to try to prevent the cub from ripping my nose off. The cub was doing much the same. This was it. I knew one of us would have to have some relief soon. So I reached around the tree with my free arm and grabbed the cub by the back of the neck and jerked him away from the tree.

He started clawing my hand, trying to get loose. He was doing some damage too, but I couldn't drop him until the guys with the catch net were ready. I couldn't let go of the tree either, or we'd both fall. I was hugging the tree with one hand and the clawing cub with the other, yelling to the people on the ground to hurry and get the net stretched out.

I gripped the cub for as long as I could stand it, then I shouted

"Get ready, here he comes!"

At that point, I released him and Les made an unplanned dive toward the net. As he fell, his front and back legs were stretched out in all directions as far as possible, like a skydiver. The little cub landed right in the center of the catch net. The rangers wrapped him up and quickly put him into a transfer cage with no harm to Les.

I climbed down from the tree with my knees shaking from adrenalin and exertion and hand bleeding from the cub's claws. I walked over to the cage to see the little bear. He looked much smaller in the cage than he had in the face-to-face encounter in the top of the tree.

When he saw me, he raised the hair up on the back of his neck and started bluff charging me from inside the cage, so I knew we had a bear with a strong will to live. Les was a survivor and would do well.

We kept Les all summer and fed him until his weight increased enough to give him the best chance to survive. When we returned him to the wild, he dashed out of the transfer cage, and then stopped to look back at us. I'm not sure what was running through his head but I hoped he was, in his own way, thanking us for helping him through a tough situation.

We hope and pray that Les was able to live a good and productive life. There were no other reports about him, and that's a good thing.

When I first saw Les up in the top of the Silverbell tree and the pool of blood from his mother on the ground, I didn't know what his fate would be. But when I saw him run out of the transfer cage, free again, I was glad we'd given him a second chance to live as a wild bear. And I realized I'd found my calling in life.

TALKING TRASH

GOOD SCIENCE-BASED BEAR MANAGEMENT was in its infancy in the late 1970s and early 1980s. We were on a pretty steep learning curve. We did a lot of things then that we wouldn't do the same way now. We did our best, but no one had the knowledge we have nowadays.

For example, we used to move a lot of bears from one place to another. Any bear that got into the habit of coming into proximity with people, we captured and took farther into the Park woods, away from the visitors' areas.

Once we moved thirty-two bears from Chimneys picnic area during a three-year period.

Since then we've learned that the fault usually lies with people, not the bears. The biggest problem is that people leave garbage out where bears can get to it. It's especially bad if the garbage is left out overnight. Nighttime garbage or trash left where it's available to bears actually starts the whole process of wild bears becoming a bigger problem later.

Now that we know this, we deal with the garbage and *talk trash* with the visitors. And now the number of bears we move outside the Park or even outside the bear's home territory is only a fraction of the number we moved in the old days.

One Sunday afternoon, I got a report about a bear at Cosby Campground. Burt Bradley, our Dispatcher, was camped there and called to let us know there was a problem. So I hopped into what we refer to as the *Elk Calf*, a Chevy S-10 pickup truck, and drove over to see what was going on.

When you first arrive on a scene it's easy to tell if a bear is active in the area. All you have to do is drive around looking for either a bear or a crowd of people with cameras all pointed in the same direction. In this case, I saw the crowd first, which is usually the case.

Cosby Campground sits on a slight incline beside Cosby Creek. A bear was clearly visible foraging close by. I estimated the bear's size at about 125 pounds, so I drew up 1 ½ cc's of immobilization drugs. We use 1 cc per 50 pounds of bear when we're in a free-range bear capture situation. We use less if the bear is in a trap because it won't require as much to subdue an animal that has already been contained.

I used a cocktail of Xylazine and Ketamine. Xylazine is a sedative, muscle relaxant, anesthesia, and analgesic sold by Bayer under the name *Rompun*. Ketamine is an anesthetic and the primary drug we use in capturing wild animals. We use both drugs together when capturing wild bears. Ketamine is also sometimes used on humans, by humans. It's what is commonly known as a date rape drug. That's one of the reasons it's controlled by the Drug Enforcement Agency.

I loaded the dart and slipped it into our Palmer Cap-Chur CO2 pistol. We use a pistol to dart bears that are within ten yards. If they're farther away, we normally have to use a more powerful gun, like a rifle.

I casually walked up to the bear, trying to look good and do everything perfectly because I had a large audience. I lined up a great shot, pulled the trigger, and the gun popped. The bear moved a little distance away, but stayed where everyone could see him, continuing to forage, looking none the worse for wear. People in the crowd were glancing at me, wondering when the bear would fall over.

A sick feeling crept over me. The sound of the gun firing hadn't been quite right. I didn't see the dart hit the bear in the rear quarter. *Where had the dart gone?* I reviewed my actions and realized I must've failed to keep the dart gun level when I was carrying it from the truck. The CO2 pistol has a smooth barrel and the dart will fall out if you tilt it toward the ground.

I'd screwed up because I'd focused more on trying to look cool and professional. In all the excitement of performing for the crowd I'd forgotten to hold the end of the gun barrel up. The dart had fallen out of the pistol somewhere along the way during my strut to take the shot. Now my problem was trying to retrieve the dart and reload the pistol without anyone realizing my dumb mistake.

"I must've missed," I said loud enough for everyone to hear, lying through my teeth. They all looked at me in disappointment. "I need to go back to my truck and reload another dart," I said. "Be back in a minute."

At least the second half of what I said was true, so I headed back to my truck.

Along the way back, I saw the dart lying on the ground so I casually bent down and picked it up as inconspicuously as possible. Then I went through an elaborate and totally fake ritual of reloading the dart pistol, concealing what I was really doing behind my truck.

Luckily the bear didn't go far while I was fumbling around, so I was able to get it with the *second* dart and everything worked out fine. There were plenty of lessons about working with wildlife—and with people—that I was going to have to learn. I learned a couple of important ones that day.

The first lesson was, if you point the dart pistol toward the ground, the dart will fall out. The second lesson was that I needed to be honest with the people who were watching. I was still in the greenhorn stage of my career and it didn't take much to shake my confidence. I knew I'd continue to make mistakes, but I promised myself I'd learn from them. I also promised myself that I'd be honest with people about whatever happened.

I was still a work in progress.

BEARS 1, MAN 0

WE TRY OUR BEST, but we can't always keep bears away from people. And we can't always keep people away from bears. There are half a million acres of Park, most of it wilderness; roughly 1,600 bears; and over nine million visitors a year.

So, it's not possible to keep an eye on it all, especially in Cades Cove. That's the most popular area of the Park. To me, it's God's country, and it's my favorite part of the Park. Two million people a year congregate there because it's such a paradise.

Lots of people compressed in close proximity to lots of bears means quite a few human-bear encounters happen there. One of the more memorable of these occurred when a momma bear was grubbing with her three cubs on the exit side of the Cades Cove Loop Road. A naïve and half-baked fellow from Alabama decided to get a picture of the bear family. Unfortunately he wasn't satisfied with a picture taken from the road where all the other visitors were clustered safely viewing the wildlife.

He wanted a close-up and he made a plan. He decided that rather than walking straight up to the bear family, he'd do an end run, go past them, and double back. He set out through the thick woods, maneuvering closer and closer, until he popped up over a log and suddenly found himself right on top of the family of bears.

Both the bears and the man were surprised and startled. The mother bear made blowing noises and popping sounds with her jaws, trying to scare him away. Her tactic worked great. The man knew he was in trouble. He turned and ran away as fast as he could go.

The fellow wasn't able to leave the area quickly enough to suit the mother bear, though, so she ran after him and lunged and shoved him in the back. The blow from the mother bear knocked him onto a dead fallen tree that had some broken off limbs. He impaled himself in a delicate area. A *very* delicate area.

He managed to get his private parts loose from the pointed tree limbs, but now he was in a lot of pain and needed some medical attention. More than anything, he just wanted to get out of Cades Cove, but he was hurt seriously enough to need help, so he went to find a ranger.

The first ranger he encountered was a female who worked at the campground kiosk. He didn't want to reveal his problem to her, so he asked her for the closest male ranger. He was willing to display the injury to a man. A male ranger evaluated the wounds and agreed that the fellow definitely needed medical attention. He got the injured man to a hospital where he was stitched up.

The visitor broke the law by approaching the bears too closely, and he got to experience some rough justice. No action was taken against the mother bear because she'd been provoked. Several of us secretly wished we had more mother bears like her scattered all over the Park.

The bears won on that one. The mother bear didn't bite the man and she didn't scratch him. She was a good bear, a good mother. She handled the problem the best way she could. She didn't do more than she thought was necessary to protect her cubs, and at the same time she gave the man a lesson he's not likely to forget. We need more momma bears like her and fewer people like him.

SKUNKED

SKUNKS PRESENT UNIQUE HAZARDS to wildlife wranglers. Their inborn defense system is so well-constructed they have virtually no natural predators. They don't have to be mean or tricky or worry about much of anything.

That's why I was worried when the Park Superintendent directed me to remove all of the food-conditioned and habituated skunks from the Cades Cove Campground. There were nearly a hundred of them living there and I had no idea how to capture them without getting me and lots of other people sprayed. As I pondered tactics, I flashed back to my college days when I'd had a bad experience with a skunk. It was not a pleasant memory.

As part of my new major, after I changed from Animal Science to Wildlife and Fisheries Science, I got a homework assignment in Mammals class. We were required to make a *museum mount*, which is essentially a tanned animal skin stuffed with cotton or newspaper.

Dr. Michael Pelton, the world famous black bear expert, was the instructor. He suggested I prepare a skunk mount because he didn't have any of those yet. I thought, *Great, a skunk it will be.* I like skunks, from a distance, and I think their coats are cool looking.

Dr. Pelton's classroom was referred to as *The Head Room* because it was full of shoulder-mounted wild animals from all over the world. After I got my assignment, I looked around the room and, sure enough, saw there were no skunk mounts anywhere. I was proud to think that I'd have the first one. I guess I wanted to impress everybody.

Of course there's an obvious problem when trying to work with skunks. You have to find a way to deal with the possibility of getting sprayed or rupturing their scent sac. I asked Dad for advice. "Son, they say if you skin one underwater," he said, "it won't spray or leak out any of its odorous dynamite."

I looked at him thinking he was kidding me, but he didn't laugh or smile. So I decided he was serious.

Dad frequently quotes things *they* say. I've never been sure who *they* are. But I've always trusted my Dad, so I went and got a five gallon bucket and filled it full of water. Then I submerged a dead skunk. It was tricky using an extremely sharp knife to skin an animal underwater. It's not easy above water, but with the animal underwater, I couldn't see what I was doing. I tried anyway, as slowly and carefully as I could.

Just when I thought things were going well, I looked down and noticed a cluster of small bubbles floating to the surface. One quick sniff and I yelled, "Whoa!" and did a backwards somersault off the inverted bucket I was using as a stool. I was the victim of a post-mortem attack. The skunk might as well have been alive. He got his revenge on me. The stench was terrible. I needed to get the corpse away from the house *fast*.

At the time my ride was a 1969 VW Beetle painted school bus yellow. I grabbed the stinking bucket, jumped in my yellow Doodle Bug, and drove across the pasture with my eyes watering, holding the bucket out the window until I got to a place where I could toss it away and go back to the house for a long hot shower.

For my class homework, I ended up mounting a gray squirrel. Dr. Pelton still doesn't have a skunk mount in his classroom and now I know why.

When I confronted Dad about the deficiency in the bit of folk wisdom he'd passed along, he admitted he'd also been the victim of some bad advice about skunks.

He said years earlier he and a friend were trying to remove a skunk from a ground den near the house. He'd heard somewhere that if you wanted to pull a skunk out of a burrow without getting sprayed, you could do it if you built a small fire in front of the den entrance and when you snatched the skunk out, you *drew it quickly across the fire*, whatever that meant.

This made no sense, but Dad and one of his friends tried it anyway. They went to the skunk burrow, built a little fire in front of it, then Dad squatted down on one side of the den entrance and reached in carefully. As soon as he started pulling the skunk out by its tail, it sprayed, as anyone with good sense could've predicted. The stink was bad enough, but to Dad's amazement, when the skunk spray shot across the fire, the methane in it ignited and the spray exploded into furling tongues of flame several feet long.

It was like a fire breathing dragon except the fire was coming out of the wrong end.

Dad and his buddy were shocked. They'd accidentally invented a new kind of hillbilly weapon that put the *spud gun* to shame. They'd discovered the skunk-powered flamethrower.

SMELLING TROUBLE—
ELVIS AND PRISCILLA

SKUNK ISSUES continued to plague me as a wildlife ranger. One day I got a call from a hiker who'd stayed at Icewater Springs Shelter the night before. He reported that skunks were living under the bunks inside the shelter. This was a cause for concern, not just on account of odors, but because skunks are the number one carrier of rabies.

The critters needed to be moved out. Luckily I had a little seniority by this time, so I asked Chuck Hester and Rick Varner if they'd be willing to tackle the job. Although they weren't extremely excited about the request, they agreed to do it.

Campers had regularly fed the animals so they had little fear of humans. They'd walk over the top of people inside the shelter as they were lying in their sleeping bags. Two of the skunks were so tame, they'd been named Elvis and Priscilla.

Chuck and Rick took a gunny sack and a couple of *Blow-Jector* blowguns made of a four-foot-long piece of metal tubing with a mouthpiece. They loaded them with 50mm pneumatic darts, called *Pneu-Darts* and used the animal tranquilizer Ketamine.

We had limited, and I mean *very* limited, experience darting skunks, but we figured skunks went through progressive behavioral changes just like bears. At first they'd be fearful, then they'd gradually they lose their fear, until eventually they'd be totally comfortable around humans.

A skunk is less likely to spray if it's not afraid. Generally, only fearful ones spray. But spraying or not, Elvis and Priscilla had to go. The plan was for the wildlife rangers to go to the shelter and eat lunch, then when the skunks came over for scraps, they could catch them.

The skunk capturing team hadn't been there ten minutes when one of the skunks came right up to them. They weren't sure if it was Elvis or Priscilla, but they darted it and put it in a sack. It looked like it was going to be easy. The rangers walked around looking for the other skunk until Rick heard some squealing noises coming from underneath the bunks.

The front sill of the bunks is a big log that lies on the ground, but there was a hollow space behind it. Rick could see a little hole in the corner. He used the small shovel kept at the shelter to enlarge the hole so he could shine a light in and illuminate the crawl space.

Sure enough, there was a skunk in there, under the cabin, so Rick used his blowgun on it and it went to sleep. But then he had to wriggle underneath the bunk to get hold of the critter and pull it out. He managed to squeeze through the small opening and grab the sleeping skunk. Then he called out to Chuck and asked him to grab hold of his ankles and pull him out.

Chuck dragged Rick out and he brought the skunk out with him. When he got the animal out into the light they saw it was a tiny baby skunk instead of the adult they expected, so Rick went back underneath the cabin and discovered there were more. *Many more.* By mid-afternoon Rick and Chuck had pulled out thirteen baby skunks. They relocated the family to a remote area of the Park.

The next day Rick and Chuck hiked back up to the shelter with a better shovel and dug out a bigger hole and Rick crawled back underneath the cabin, this time wearing a respirator and safety glasses. The rangers worked until they'd dragged out all the garbage the skunks had cached under the floor. Each time Rick got a bag full, he'd yell for Chuck to drag him out by the ankles.

The skunk crew collected nine bags of garbage from underneath the cabin. By the end of the day, they both smelled strongly of skunk and garbage. Some of the tasks of a wildlife ranger are harder than others.

THE GOOD, BUT STINKY, SAMARITAN

SOMEONE AT THE SUGARLANDS called Dispatch and said there was a skunk wandering around the Visitor Center parking lot with its head stuck in mayonnaise jar. Dispatch said they'd notify Wildlife, which meant me. They radioed, asking for *340*, which was my call number.

Being able to predict the ultimate result of grabbing a skunk and pulling a mayonnaise jar off its head caused me to hesitate to answer the call for help. When I didn't answer immediately, the North District Ranger, Don Utterbak, whose office is in the Visitor Center, called back to Dispatch and said he'd check on the skunk.

Whew, I'd dodged a bullet there, for sure. Poor Don. The Sugarlands Visitor Center is one of the busiest places in the Park, so a lot of tourists were standing around, watching to see who was going to show up and deal with the skunk.

In one way Don was successful. He ran the skunk down, grabbed the jar, and managed to remove it from the skunk's head. The skunk didn't fully appreciate his efforts, though, because it blasted Don at point blank range in front of the crowd of tourists.

The he came into Headquarters to commiserate with his colleagues about what had happened. He didn't need to say anything, though. He couldn't disguise the results of his encounter with the skunk. The odor was so strong that everyone immediately scattered. There was no one left to talk to, so Don went home. No one got to hear his story.

The price for being a Good Samaritan can be pretty high. And lonely.

THE GREAT SKUNK RODEO

THE GO-TO GUY for tough wildlife jobs is Rick Varner. Rick is a former U.S. Marine. He's brave, smart, strong, quiet, thorough, and totally reliable. Rick is a cross between Rambo and MacGyver. There isn't anything he can't do and nothing he's afraid of trying.

He's a meticulous planner who takes advance measures to avert disaster. He mentally prepares for difficult situations before he starts a task, dotting all the i's and crossing all the t's. So whenever we were given a task that was nearly impossible, or bound to be extraordinarily unpleasant, or challenging, or difficult, I called on Rick. One of these times was what came to be known as *The Great Skunk Rodeo in Cades Cove.*

For many years, the most popular wildlife attraction in the Cades Cove campground was a herd of skunks. The technical term for a gang of skunks is a *surfeit*. Countless generations of these skunks had been born and raised amid a swirling mass of tourists, RVs, cars, and tents.

Skunks have few natural enemies aside from a few birds of prey with a nearly non-existent sense of smell. This happy fact, in conjunction with year-round access to visitors' food and garbage, resulted in a population explosion. The cove campground was truly skunk heaven.

Inevitably, skunks occupying the same area as visitors are an accident waiting to happen—and one did. On a weekend when the campground was full, I got a call at home saying a young boy had been bitten by a skunk and since the responsible skunk wasn't captured, the little boy was going to have to get post-exposure rabies shots.

It happened that the little boy's father worked for the National Park Service in the Washington Office. So, news about the incident ran quickly through the National Park Service ranks. On the

Monday morning following the incident, Superintendent John Cook was sitting in my office when I got to work. That didn't happen very often.

From the look on John's face, I knew the Cades Cove campground skunks were about to get a new home. We knew the best option for the skunks was to relocate them to a less populated area where the health of both tourists and skunks would be better protected.

We decided to take the skunks several miles away from the cove, across a ridge, and into another watershed. But first we had to devise a sneaky way of catching them and suppressing their spraying defense. There was no known technique for how to do this.

After much thought, we decided to use blowguns to subdue the skunks and the *boar*, a powerful Dodge 4x4 pickup truck fitted with a wild hog cage in the back, for transport. Small darts carrying 1 cc of animal tranquilizer, shot from blowguns, would knock the skunks unconscious for a couple of hours. We figured that would be more than enough time to drive them ten miles to a new home at Sams Gap on Parsons Branch Road.

The skunks never saw it coming. Rick and I started our walk through the campground one evening, puffed little darts at each of the skunks, and down they went. When I bent over to pick up our first critter, Rick told me there was a trick to handling unconscious skunks.

"Skunks can't spray unless their tail is up in the air," he said. "The tail *has* to be folded down over the rear end of the skunk when you pick em up, even when they're asleep, or the scent can leak out. But they can't get you if you keep that tail locked down."

This sounded ominously similar to my Dad's famous last words about how to hold the tail of a cow to keep her from kicking your brains out. I hoped Rick's advice would work out better than Dad's.

As quickly as we could, we walked from one end of the campground to the other, blow-darting skunks. But, even working as fast as possible, by the time we were darting the last of the skunks, the ones who'd been darted first were starting to wake up.

This wasn't a good situation.

So, even though we hadn't captured *all* the skunks, we decided we already had *enough* skunks—possibly more than we could handle. Seventy-seven skunks seemed like a good night's work. And we figured we'd better not wait any longer before moving them. A truckload of angry drunk skunks wasn't something we wanted to deal with.

When we finally got them all loaded, Rick took pity on me and volunteered to drive the skunks to their new home by himself. That's just the way Rick is. "There's no reason for both of us to get sprayed," he said, the brave Marine to the bitter end.

I agreed to let him martyr himself. It was shortly after midnight when he slammed the tailgate and took off. I watched him drive away, worried about how the evening would end for him. I'd learned the hard way that strategies for wildlife management rarely go as planned.

The next day when I got to work I expected to be able to smell Rick before I could see him, but that wasn't the case. He was at work before I got there, which was the norm, looking fresh and bright as always.

"How'd it go?" I asked.

"As I went around the Loop Road," Rick said, "I glanced in the rear view mirror and saw a skunk rared up against the side of the truck bed, trying to look out. I was pretty surprised to see that one of em had managed to get outta the cage.

"I kept checking in the mirror as I drove and more and more of the rascals were getting out. In a few minutes, a row of little black and white heads was lining both sides of the truck bed.

"I figured there must be a hole in the cage and decided I better fix it, so I stopped the truck and went back to take a look at what was going on. Well, at least half the skunks were awake and they were milling around, coming and going through the chain link cage with no trouble at all.

"Only then did I remember that skunks are members of the *weasel* family. They're *all hair*! But there was nothing I could do about it, so I jumped back in the truck and took off again.

"As I drove, more and more of em woke up until it looked like *all* of em were outta the cage, rared up, looking out over the sides of the truck.

"My original plan had been to get to the new location while all the skunks were still asleep, lay em out on the ground, and then take off before they woke up. But now, I needed a new plan.

"Let me tell you, seventy-seven skunks is a boatload. And every one of them was wide awake by the time I got to Sam's Gap. I was afraid to grab any of em for fear they'd spray me, so there was nothing else to do, but park the *boar* with the back of it downhill, jerk the tailgate open, and run.

"So that's what I did.

"I watched from about ten yards away while the skunks milled around in the bed of the truck. Some of them glanced over the edge of the tailgate outta curiosity, but not a single one jumped out. So, I waited some more.

"Then I realized I'd never actually seen a skunk jump. I wondered if maybe they didn't know how to jump. Maybe they were *never* going to be able to jump outta the truck. I waited a little longer to be sure, but it was getting really late.

"I decided to build a ramp for them to walk down, so I looked around for some logs or something. But I couldn't find anything to use. By this time it was nearly three in the morning and I was tired. It'd been a really long day.

"I sneaked up to the back of the truck and watched for a flash of white near the edge of the tailgate. When I saw it, I snatched the skunk by the tail and tossed it to the ground. I did it again and again, every time one of em came near the edge of the tailgate. It took a long time. But because they're so tame, they never did get scared or mad at me.

"After I'd off-loaded the last one, I turned to go get in the truck and felt something on my boots. I looked down and there was this huge cluster of skunks at my feet. Not *one* of them had run off.

"It dawned on me that they'd been raised around people and underneath campers, so they didn't think of the woods or a field as home. They were staying underneath the truck or right next to me because that was all they knew!

"It was surreal. Skunk's eyes glow really bright at night and they were staring at me. I shuffled through them to get to the driver's door, got in, and started the *boar*. I eased away, creeping along until I'd gotten away from them. It wasn't hard, skunks don't move very fast.

"I could see all those glowing eyes in the rear view mirror, then I floored it and got outta there so fast there was no way they could follow me. And I never did get sprayed."

Interesting Skunk Fact

Although nobody got sprayed during the relocation process, several hours later the *boar* and Rick and I all began to smell like skunk anyway.

Rick and I washed everything really well and Cloroxed our hands several times.

The skunk smell would go away for a while, then it would come back. This fading and re-appearing of the smell went on for about two weeks. It was crazy.

Rick mentioned it to me and remarked that there was no odor in the morning, but it came back at about two in the afternoon and then again at about six at night. I said the same thing had been happening to me!

Well, it turns out that brass is oily and absorbs odors. Our Park Service belt buckles are made of brass. Our hands and clothes were clean, but after we touched our belt buckles a few times during the day, our hands were picking up the skunk smell again.

So, we soaked our ranger badges and belt buckles in Clorox and that solved the problem at least for our hardware. Twenty-five years later, my wife still swears that she smells skunk when I sweat. So, in consideration of my wife, I do my best to never sweat anymore.

THE DENIM DEER

WHEN CAPTURING THE PARK'S wild critters with drugs to either relocate them, doctor them, or collect samples, we often blindfold it to help keep it calm while we work. When the animal is fully under the effects of the drugs it loses the ability to blink, so we cover its eyes to protect them. The blindfold also helps reduce an animal's fright as it is waking up with us holding it or standing nearby. We do this mainly when working with deer, elk, and bear.

Once we were capturing deer for Lyme disease monitoring in Cades Cove. We needed to catch around fifty deer in a week, so we developed a system for handling them. Dr. New, from the University of Tennessee Veterinary Hospital, cut the leg off a pair of his old blue jeans to use as a blindfold.

We'd captured an adult female deer, called a *doe*, near Sparks Lane and loaded her in the transport truck with Dr. New and his crew. Apparently the deer didn't get as much drug as we'd hoped and she needed a bit more to get her into a sound sleep state. As they drove the truck back to the animal workup area at the horse barn, she unexpectedly woke up in the back of the *Sow*, a Chevy extended cab pickup truck.

Dr. New was holding her and she was still wearing the denim blindfold. The doe began to struggle and Dr. New and his helpers couldn't hold her down. She leaped up and they grabbed at the blindfold but, instead of getting it off, they only succeeded in pulling it down onto her neck.

Fabric slides down an animal's neck pretty easily, but it's a lot harder to remove because then you're pulling opposite to the way the hair grows. So, despite the handlers' best efforts, the deer escaped wearing the blindfold around her neck. From that point on, everywhere she went, she was wearing what looked like a denim scarf or blue jean collar.

We tried for days to recapture the deer, but she remembered the ordeal she'd just experienced and wouldn't let anyone get within a mile of her. We received endless calls from visitors who reported a deer running around with a blue neck. Fortunately, the denim necklace posed no health issues for the animal.

We tried to put a positive spin on the situation and said she was the best dressed deer in Cades Cove. The *Denim Deer* eventually settled down enough so that we were able to catch her and remove the blue jean collar. After that, her attire was back to casual. Blue just wasn't her color.

SOMETHING'S IN MY PANTS

THE DIRTIEST I EVER GOT in the backcountry was when I was working a forest fire. Rangers from all over the country volunteered to help fight a big wildfire in a wilderness area in Oregon a few years after the eruption of Mt. St. Helens.

The National Park Service divided the volunteers into twenty-person fire crews and flew us out west. We were far enough away from Mt. St. Helens that the blast from the volcano hadn't flattened the trees, but the ash cloud from the eruption had completely blanketed the ground between the trees and it was still there when the forest fire started.

So, all day we were walking through the volcanic ash or struggling up steep slopes with the ash running downhill along the trails like a thick soup. The ash covered everything and infiltrated everything—our clothes, packs, sinuses, and lungs. Everyone was absolutely filthy.

Being in a large firefighting camp is an interesting experience. It's loud and chaotic with hundreds of firefighters and support staff running in all directions. Helicopters and planes are flying overhead, dropping water and supplies. We were each assigned to a crew that we'd eat, sleep, and work with throughout the entire ordeal. We normally worked sixteen hour shifts so working, eating, and sleeping filled up the day.

Before the camp was fully set up, at night I'd jump into a small creek to wash off. We weren't supposed to do that for fear of microscopic parasites in the water, but I couldn't stand being so grungy. Later they brought in large tractor trailers that had been modified to provide showers.

Firefighters stood outside the trailers wearing towels, waiting their turn. Obviously, the girls had their own shower trailer. When you went inside, the middle of the trailer was rigged with several water hoses. You picked one of these up off the floor to use to take your shower.

If the sight of a bunch of grimy, naked guys crammed into an eighteen-wheeler with water, dirt, and soap splattering everywhere wasn't enough, the smell was certainly something I'll never forget, although I'd like to. It reminded me of my old football playing days after a long hard practice and the unforgettable sweaty and pungent smell of the locker room—times ten.

After we showered, which got us only slightly cleaner, we ate. The food is the best part of a fire camp—you're extremely well fed, or so it always seemed to me. But maybe any kind of food tastes great when you're that hungry. The first night, the crew I was assigned to unrolled our sleeping bags and tried to bed down, knowing we wouldn't get much sleep because we had to get up at 4:30 in the morning and start the long day all over again.

My legs and back were so stiff I could hardly move. My shoulders and hands were sore from digging fire lines all day. I never dreamed I could sleep so well lying on the side of a hill with no mattress or pillow, but I did. Obviously, if you're tired enough, you can sleep just about anywhere.

When I woke up the next morning I climbed out of my bag in the pre-dawn darkness and stretched as much as possible to try and get all my parts working again. Before I'd gone to bed the night before, I'd hung my fire pants on a low limb of a pine tree in the hope they'd dry out a little bit overnight.

I had to prop myself against the pine tree for balance as I struggled to put on my pants. They were green and made of Nomex, a stiff, bulky, fire-retardant material. When I pulled them up, I suddenly felt something bouncing around inside them, hitting me in the rear end and other sensitive parts.

"Len, get your flashlight," I gasped to my good friend, Len

Weems. "Something's alive in my pants!"

Len quickly turned his flashlight on as I lowered the pants to my knees to see what it was. At the exact moment his flashlight found the front of my fire pants, a chipmunk leaped from inside one of the legs onto my open fly, and just stopped there momentarily to take a look around, with his head sticking out and his two front paws clinging onto my zipper.

I stood there, frozen, with my pants halfway up, waiting for the chipmunk to make the first move. The scared chipmunk looked at Len, then at me, and made a high-pitched chirp. Then, after a momentary hesitation, he leaped out of my pants and scurried away.

Obviously the chipmunk had decided to sleep inside my pants while I wasn't using them, but it got too crowded in there when I tried to put them on. I was extremely lucky that the little rascal hadn't bitten me in the butt or somewhere worse.

"That woulda been somethin if you'd gotten bit and got an infection and had to be sent home," Len said. "You'd be ridin the bus with other injured firefighters, men who had cuts, broken bones, and dislocated joints. You'd probably have to lie if somebody asked you how you got hurt. I can't picture you sayin, "Chipmunk bit my %^&*#!"

Fortunately I didn't have to face that humiliation, but Len and the others in my crew got a good laugh to start their day off. I suspect the chipmunk had a good story to tell when he got home, too.

CLIMBING UNDER THE INFLUENCE

BECAUSE THE SMOKIES have such a high density of both bears and visitors, bruins and humans often cross paths.

In the early days after the Park was created in 1934, rangers were forced to kill bears because they didn't have the experience to know what to do with them when they started panhandling or going into populated areas getting aggressive and causing problems.

Later, after we learned to install bear-proof trash cans, that helped tremendously, although the problem wasn't completely solved. Nuisance bears still sought handouts from visitors and neighbors.

The key to understanding all the mistakes we made in the early days, and why we made them, is that back then there was no book explaining how to capture a black bear, or a family of bears, in the wild. We learned everything the painful way, by trial and error. We made a lot of goofs. But we also got some things right.

It's nearly impossible to always predict what a wild animal is going to do, especially when you're trying to catch the critter. For example, at Cosby Campground we had a panhandling bear that had been in the campground for several weeks causing chaos with the visitors, so the decision was made capture and move it.

It was Monday morning and my boss, Bill Cook, told me to go to Cosby to see if I could catch the bear and bring it back to Headquarters. Any time your boss asks you to do something that they've never actually done themselves, all sorts of unexpected things can happen. At this point I'd darted a few bears by myself but I wasn't really that proficient yet. Well, I sure got some additional experience on this assignment.

When I got to Cosby, the big bear was already moving through the campground with an entourage of people closely following him wherever he went. I estimated the bear to be around 250 pounds, so I used five cc's of our drug cocktail (1 cc per 50 pounds of bear). I positioned myself for a good close shot and pulled the trigger. The dart hit directly in the center of the bear's hip. I thought all I had to do was wait until the bear went to sleep, load him up, and I'd be done!

But, that ain't the way it happened.

This bear had been harried by people so intensely that he'd had just about all he could take, so when the dart hit him, he ran to one of the biggest poplar trees in the campground and climbed fifty feet up the tree so fast that it looked like he was riding in an elevator. Standing there in shock, all I could think was, *Ohhhhhh crap!*

I'd never darted an adult bear that had then climbed a tree, and especially not that high up. All the others had stayed on the ground. *What am I supposed to do now?*, I wondered. There must've been seventy-five people staring at me, waiting to see what I was going to do next.

I knew if I was trying to catch a bear and it jumped onto the side of a tree, that was a clue that it might try to escape vertically, so everyone should back off immediately and give the animal time and space to settle down. But this bear had been on the ground when I shot it. It had given no indication it might climb a tree. But as soon as I darted it, it ran five stories straight up.

This is really, really bad, I thought.

If the bear went to sleep in the top of that tree and fell fifty feet, the fall would kill it and I'd be responsible for its death. Not a good feeling. Not knowing anything else to do, I turned and yelled for everyone to go back to their campsites *now* so the bear could feel safe enough to come down out of the tree.

"Get in your cars and go," I yelled forcefully to the crowd. To be honest, I made them leave not only so the bear might feel comfortable enough to come down on her own, but also because I didn't want them to see what happened, in case things went awry.

As I watched, I could see the bear was beginning to succumb to the drugs. I watched her helplessly as she swayed, clinging to the side of the tree high in the air. She managed to hold on for a long time. Gradually her head began to loll backwards, but still she was able to hang on to the side of the tree.

After another minute her grip began to relax and she slid about ten feet down the trunk of the tree. *Uh oh, this is it,* I thought. But she held onto the side of the tree and stopped her fall. Then she did it again, her head lolled backwards and she slid another ten feet down the trunk before she was able to rouse enough to grab hold again. She did this several times.

Finally her head rolled back, her claws gave way, and she fell backwards off the tree, but by that time she was only about five feet off the ground, so she was fine. I looked around and several people had snuck back and were still watching. One of them yelled, "Ranger, how'd you know that bear would slide down the tree and not fall off?"

I wanted to say, *Sir, when you've done this as long as I have, you just know.* But, with my knees still shaking, I said, "Sir, I didn't know. I guess my Guardian Angel was with me and the bear today."

I gave a big sigh of relief and walked toward the sleeping bear thinking, *Thank you Lord up above.*

THE ELK THIEF

I'M SUPPOSED TO BE ABLE to explain animal behavior to the public. That's a big part of a wildlife ranger's job. But sometimes I have no earthly idea why animals do the things they do.

Elk #3, in particular, caused a problem I never saw coming and had no good explanation for. Elk #3 was the first of the elk to travel on its own over to Oconaluftee from Cataloochee. In fact, he made the trip several times a year. It's about a ten-mile straight line trek each way.

David Ensley, a big 6' 3" guy, headed the Game and Fish Department for the Eastern Band of Cherokee Indians. One day he called me about a report of an elk stealing a quilt from an elderly lady in Big Cove on the Cherokee Indian Reservation. The elk apparently snatched a quilt off the lady's back porch and ran away with it.

I thought someone had to be mistaken. Why would an elk have any interest in stealing a quilt? But I was happy to help if I could. The next day I drove across the mountains and met with David in his office. He brought me up to date, then said, "Come on," he said, "let's go talk to her." So we did.

She was a frail Cherokee lady in her 80's. She said it was bull Elk #3. She knew exactly which elk it was because she'd seen his ear tag. She said the elk stole her quilt right after she'd washed it, grabbing it from the railing of her back porch where she'd hung it out to dry. The elk had also walked around in her garden and slightly damaged it.

We tried, but we were unable to find her stolen quilt. Next, I went to my Dad's because he had a stockpile of electric fencing materials. I raided his supplies, and then we put up an electric fence with a gate to protect the lady's garden.

When I finished building her a fence, she asked me, "Why would that elk steal my quilt?"

"Ma'am," I said, "I have no earthly idea why he did that. It doesn't make any sense."

"I heard something," she said, reviewing the odd scenario in her mind, "and I went out onto the back porch and I saw that elk grab my quilt. When he noticed me, he ran off with a corner of the quilt in his mouth. He carried it all the way across the field with it flying out behind him in the wind, like a cape. The last I saw of it was when he disappeared with it into the woods."

She looked at me for an explanation. I was the big wildlife expert after all. All I could do was repeat, "Ma'am, I don't know why he did that." I told her I'd do my best to find it for her, and I looked in the woods for it again, but I never saw any trace of it. Later, in more fanciful moments, I wondered if the elk might be wearing it on cold winter nights.

Despite the occasional annoyances caused by the new elk, the Cherokee were very supportive of the elk program and have helped me and the animals any way they could.

When a new Cherokee school near the Park boundary was nearly completed, along with a new football stadium, early one morning, laborers arrived for work to find three young bull elk standing casually in the middle of the new football field, directly atop the freshly-painted school logo, as if ready to flip a coin to see who'd kick off and who'd receive the football.

This intrusion was graciously forgiven.

With elk as the "new kids on the block" at the reservation we were worried at first that people might try to kill them, but that didn't happen. It was quite the opposite, in fact.

When one of the large bull elk went to Big Cove near where some Cherokee people live, a wildlife researcher was attempting to find it. The researcher was tuning her tracking antenna when a very large, tough-looking fellow came running out of a nearby house and wanted to know what she was doing. "Are you trying to catch the elk and take em outta here?" he asked.

"No," she said, "I'm only trying to find em to be sure they're okay."

"Well, leave em here," he told her. "Don't take em outta here."

The man was very protective of the elk. That surprised us. People had a huge list of preconceived ideas about the problems elk would supposedly cause, but they didn't do much harm. Of course, quilt stealing and playing on the football field hadn't been on my radar as things that might happen.

But clashes like this were inevitable. If elk were going to survive in the Smokies after being gone for so long, they had to become accustomed to their new home and people had to agree to share some of the space with them.

THE ESCAPE ARTIST

I GOT A CALL from Jack Campbell, a ranger who worked at the Balsam Mountain Campground. He said they had a large male bear harassing his campers during the night. He'd tried to run the bear off, but this bear had his own ideas, and leaving the campground wasn't one of them.

I promised Jack that I'd send someone over with a culvert trap before nightfall. This type of trap is made from a seven-foot long aluminum tile or culvert that has a diameter of three feet. It has dozens of two-inch air holes cut into it that are large enough to provide excellent ventilation, but not so large as to allow the bear to break any teeth on them.

Once the bait was tied to the trigger and the door set, it didn't take long for the bear to take the bait. Then the door slammed shut, locking him in. The next morning I had someone bring the bear to the Wildlife Building. I asked Bill Stiver to put him in the ten-by-fourteen-by-six-foot chain link holding cage until we could find a good place to release him.

We have to sedate a bear to be able to safely take it out of the trap and move it into the larger holding cage in the Wildlife Building. That particular day, Bill Stiver had the honor of dealing with the big fellow and he successfully made the transfer.

Afterwards, Bill was sitting in the office next door to the room with the holding cage, on the phone with the Tennessee Wildlife Resources Agency trying to find a place to relocate the bear. He heard a strange sound coming from the room where the bear was being held and got up and peeked through the door to check it out.

What Bill saw wasn't good. It was one of those times when you don't know whether to run, yell, go home, or do it all. The big male bear was half way out of the holding cage and working his way to freedom again. He'd managed to deform the wire and create an opening large enough for his head to get through.

The bottom half of the bear was still in the cage but the upper half was outside of it. The bear was using his paws to pull himself through the hole. If a bear's head can pass through, with a little work, the rest of the body will follow. Bill slammed the door and ran across the parking lot to the wildlife lab to get an immobilization dart. Although he may've set a world record in loading a dart, the bear still managed to get out of the cage and escape from the building through the window before he got back.

Bill ran around to the front of the building where he found the big bruin climbing over an eight-foot-high chain-link fence topped with three strands of barbed wire. Bill darted the bear as it was climbing over the fence, but the impact of the dart only increased the speed of the bear's flight. It ran up the hill and vanished into the woods.

Luckily Chip Buchanan, our best animal tracker, happened to be nearby at the time. Bill called him on the radio and told him to report to the Wildlife Building *immediately*. Chip and Bill tracked the bear through the thick brush on the mountain above the Wildlife Building and were finally able to sneak up on the partially-sedated animal.

Apparently the bear hadn't absorbed the entire dose of immobilization drugs from the first dart, so Bill darted it a second time. The bear went down, but there was no way Bill and Chip could carry him out of the steep woods. Bill decided to run back and get help. Chip stayed with the bear to protect him in case other animals happened by and to help Bill and the haul crew find their way back to the bear.

It takes time to round people up and gather the necessary equipment. By the time Bill and the crew got to Chip, the drugs unfortunately had worn off enough for the bear to run away again.

Chip said there was nothing he could do. Even though the bear had burned off part of the drugs and was still a little groggy, he was able to rouse enough to make another escape.

We were all upset that the big bear had escaped, especially Bill. We didn't know if, when, or where he might strike again. Knowing that most bears try to return to their home territory, we called Ranger Jack and told him the bear had escaped and to be on the lookout, just in case he returned to the Balsam Mountain Campground. After that, all we could do was wait.

For the rest of the summer we had no reports of the big bear, but the following year, Jack called and said, "He's back. Get over here and catch him, ASAP."

The bear had traveled all the way back to his previous location to resume his foraging in the exact same place where he'd left off. The distance from the Wildlife Building to the North Carolina campground is roughly sixteen miles as the crow flies, but many more miles if you account for the steep hills and hollers in between.

This particular bear was a little intimidating to Jack, and to us, too. He was rather large, very bold, and had little fear of anyone, and I mean *anyone*. He had a history of breaking into cars for coolers, but this was in the early years when we were still learning how to deal with bad bear behaviors.

Bill went over to Balsam Mountain Campground with a trap. The big bear came in during the middle of the night, but this time he avoided the trap, even though we were using our number one secret weapon for capturing wary bears—Krispy Kreme doughnuts.

When we use doughnuts, usually a bear is sitting in the trap when we arrive the next morning, but not this ole boy. He'd already had a rather unpleasant road trip being towed in the trap on wheels and he wasn't going to make that mistake again. But shortly after he snubbed our bait, Bill was patrolling the campground and saw the bear standing on its hind feet looking into the window of a van.

There was a young girl sleeping in the van and the bear was close to popping the window out. Bill worked his way over to a place where he had a good shot and he fired his dart gun. Soon the bear was sleeping soundly.

Bill brought the bear back for his second visit to the Wildlife Building. Since we'd already ear-tagged and gathered all the information we needed on this bear, he was ready to be taken to a new home far away from the campground he'd been terrorizing.

The Tennessee Wildlife Resources Agency and the U. S. Forest Service gave the okay to release him on their property, and we took him to the Ocoee Bear Sanctuary, located on the Tennessee-Georgia state line. We released him as far south as we possibly could and still be in the State of Tennessee. We were so close to the Georgia state line that we could almost touch it.

In this remote area he'd have his best chance of living a free and wild life. Once we opened the transfer cage, the bear quickly disappeared into the brush. We never heard of him causing any problems again. He may have missed the doughnuts, but after dealing with Bill, Chip, Jack, and others, he decided the best thing for him was to remain in the wild and stay away from people. We agreed.

BEAR HUGS AND OTHER REALLY BAD IDEAS

I WAS AT HOME on a Sunday afternoon when I got a phone call like something out of my worst nightmares. Dispatch said a bear was attacking a lady at Newfound Gap and I should come immediately. Apparently the bear still had hold of the woman and wouldn't let her go.

I jumped into the *Piglet*, a four wheel drive Ford Ranger pickup truck, and raced to the Gap. The attack was happening on the border of Tennessee and North Carolina, near where the Appalachian Trail crosses Hwy. 441. It's the famous site where President Roosevelt dedicated the Park and it has a high lookout that's a popular place for tourists to stop and enjoy the view. There's a big parking lot there bounded by low stone walls.

By the time I arrived, the bear had released the lady, but he had remained close by in plain view. He was obviously very reluctant to leave the area. I was told he'd run up to an elderly lady, grabbed her by the leg, and held on to her. The crowd took immediate action by yelling and screaming and finally managed to force the bear to release the lady. They'd chased the bear away, but he hadn't gone very far.

I was shocked to hear that the bear hadn't hurt the lady at all. He hadn't bitten or even scratched her. Apparently he'd just run her down and latched onto her leg and wouldn't let go. She'd screamed and tried to get away, but the bear held on for dear life. This was strange. I had no idea why the bear would've done such a thing.

We darted and captured him to see if we could figure out what was going on. When we got a close look we saw that he had no claws. Apparently someone had surgically declawed him. The situation was starting to make a little more sense now. The bear hadn't been attacking the woman at all. He wasn't trying to get her food or hurt her in any way. He was only trying to get close to someone. He'd been someone's so-called pet.

He obviously was a captive bear that someone had hand-raised, then released into the Park. The timing of the release gave a clue as to what had probably happened. The State of North Carolina had just announced that people could no longer keep captive black bears as pets or for a business where they charged people to see and feed them. People who had a black bear in captivity would soon get a visit from the State and the animal would be confiscated.

We knew there were several individuals who'd been keeping bears in cages. So, although we never found out for sure, we strongly suspected that someone who didn't want to have their bear seized had decided to release their pet into the Park. And even worse, it looked like they might've come to the popular parking lot in the wee hours and dumped him directly into an area that would soon be crowded with visiting families and many small children.

It was a horrible, pathetic situation. There was no way a bear like that had the ability to survive in the wild. The big fellow had been raised in captivity and had no idea how to live in the wilderness. And since he had no claws, he couldn't possibly make it in the wild. He probably would've died a slow and agonizing death.

The bear had been approaching people for help, although it didn't come across that way to the tourists. He was hungry, lonely, and confused, so he had approached the crowd at the lookout and when they ran away, he ran after them and caught the first person he could. Humans had fed and cared for him up until now, and he was desperate to get help.

We couldn't relocate the bear to another place inside the Park or to the nearby National Forest because he was a captive animal and didn't have the survival skills or natural equipment, like claws, to stay alive. And he was conditioned to people and relied on them for food.

Unfortunately it looked like we were going to have to put the fellow down. I was sick over it and furious. The bear had done nothing wrong. The bear was good and gentle. Even when he was hungry and scared, he hadn't hurt anyone. But we couldn't allow a full grown pet bear to roam around loose. It was too frightening and dangerous for tourists, plus it wouldn't be humane for the bear.

Then a miracle happened. Someone who worked at the Park happened to hear that a private zoo in Parker City, Indiana had lost their big male bear to cancer and was possibly looking for another one to replace it. I researched the zoo and found out that it was a reliable place and in good standing with the Department of Agriculture, the agency responsible for permitting zoos.

Normally we couldn't take a wild bear out of the Park and send it to a zoo, but this was an extremely unusual situation. This wasn't a wild bear. We'd captured a tame bear and that was something we had zero experience with.

There was a *huge* amount of paperwork to get the bear transferred to the zoo. It was phenomenal, a bureaucratic nightmare, but we worked hard on it and eventually succeeded.

After all the permits and authorizations were in place, staff from the Parker City Zoo came down and picked up the bear and he's now living very happily there. He's visited by a lot of people who are in a position to admire him and learn about him in safety.

We got lucky that time. Sometimes things work out well despite the cruel decision-making that would cause an animal's owner to dump a captive animal into a hostile environment, turning a full grown bear into a stray animal begging for help from a crowd of unsuspecting strangers on vacation.

RUNNING WILD

MY YOUNGER BROTHER, Mike, worked with me as a wild hog hunter one summer. One night we were hunting four miles west of Clingmans Dome, near Silers Bald in the area called *The Narrows*, a distinctive ridge with a bony spine running along the top.

We'd slowly eased our way west along the Appalachian Trail to an area riddled with lots of fresh hog rooting. Soon we heard the sounds of a group of hogs plowing the dirt nearby. There's no mistaking when you hear a group of wild hogs rooting, especially when the leaf litter is dry. They're loud.

We could hear deep grunts and an occasional squeal. Every once in a while we could hear a loud blowing sound. That was a hog blowing its nose to clear the dirt. Mike and I checked the wind direction, hoping that the group wouldn't be able to smell us. A hog's vision may not be the best, but their sense of smell is excellent. The wind was blowing in our faces, so we knew we were good to go.

We started working our way closer to the group. To avoid being detected by the hogs, we walked without a light, slowly feeling our way along the trail, trying not to kick a rock or root, or trip and fall flat on our face, which we'd both done before. Once we got close enough, Mike turned his light on and I fired several shotgun blasts. Two of the destructive invaders dropped in their tracks and the others ran away. "Let's go!" I said, so we took off running after the remaining animals, trying to get close enough for another shot.

We were stumbling through dog hobble shrubs and thick briars and soon realized the hogs had disappeared over the steep slope and run off into North Carolina. All we could hear was the sound of rustling leaves and an occasional grunt from one of the retreating beasts. Running through thick vegetation isn't the smartest thing to do, especially in the dark in an area you've never been in before. Briars, beech saplings, and low-lying limbs constantly slap you in the face and scratch you as you run. You could hurt your eyes, and it's definitely not the most pleasant thing in the world, but if you want to make contact with as many of the pesky critters as possible, you go where they go.

Mike and I eventually stopped running and stood breathing heavily. Then, all of a sudden, without warning, Mike said, "Oh, %^&*#!," and took off running again in the dark.

I could tell something had scared the heebie-jeebies out of him, but he didn't take the time to explain what it was. He just took off through the woods as fast as he could go. Even though I had no idea what he was running from, his hasty exit looked serious enough that I figured we'd talk about it later. I took off after him.

Mike and I were big husky farm boys and our body makeup wasn't really suited for quick sprints. Nevertheless I can assure you that most people would've had a tough time catching either of us that night. As I was running, I could see Mike's flashlight beam. It was bouncing around all over the place, but it still gave me a clear indication of which direction to go to follow him.

Mike had bolted carrying our only flashlight and I had the only gun. For those reasons I figured I should stay with him if I could, even though he was way out in front of me. He ran for a long time and I followed his wildly bouncing light as best I could, running at maximum speed over uneven ground in almost total darkness carrying my shotgun.

When he finally stopped and I caught up to him, we were both completely out of breath again. I managed to ask him between gasps and wheezes, "What the heck happened back there?"

"I don't know," he said, panting.

"What do you mean, *you don't know*? Did you see somethin?"

"I don't know," he said.

"Did you hear somethin?"

"I told you I don't know!" he shouted, then he added, "I might've heard somethin."

"What was it?"

"I don't know!"

We were both reluctant to go back. Mike finally managed to explain that he'd heard a rustling in the leaves close to his feet. By the time we'd caught our breath, neither of us was sure we wanted to find out what it was.

I reminded him that we were way off-trail, which wasn't a good idea. We needed to get back to where we'd left the trail or risk getting turned around and lost and possibly having to call for help. That would be extremely embarrassing.

"Let's go back the way we came and maybe we'll see what it was," I suggested.

After some deep thought and some more deep breathing, Mike hesitantly agreed to go back and followed me toward where we'd been when he'd first taken flight. We traveled a *lot* slower on the way back than we had on the way out. It was quite a bit easier, too, because this time I had the benefit of the flashlight. When we found the spot where we'd both taken off, we looked around carefully and there, behind a rock, was a large boar carcass. It was one I'd shot, but obviously it had managed to run several more yards before it died, which is normal.

Apparently, when Mike and I were chasing after the fleeing herd and stopped to listen and catch our breath, Mike's leg was within inches of the dying boar. While we were standing there huffing and puffing, the boar made a final kick before it moved on to hog heaven or wherever hogs go.

When he heard the mysterious rustling in the dry leaves, it really didn't matter to Mike if it was a boar, a snake, a bear, or an elephant. His gut instinct told him to run and he did it very well. I can't poke fun at him too much because I was running right behind him. All I can say is, a man's gotta do what a man's gotta do.

By the time we found the trail it was around two o'clock in the morning. We were both exhausted, but we still had a long walk to reach our camp at Silers Bald for some much needed rest and shut-eye. Our luck held and we made it back to our tent, and were able to catch a few hours sleep before we had to get back up, go back out, and do it all over again.

UNDERWEAR ON THE TRAIL

HIKERS WERE MAKING REPORTS at ranger stations saying a bear was causing serious problems for backpackers at Silers Bald, and, at times, getting inside the shelter. Silers Bald Shelter is located on the Appalachian Trail about four and a half miles west of the Clingmans Dome parking area.

A bear trying to get in was, of course, scary to people trying to sleep inside the shelter. It's terrifying to be trapped and cowering in a small enclosed space separated from a large wild animal by only a chain link fence. Especially if the fence has been compromised by wear and tear and damaged from previous efforts of animals trying to get in.

Apparently some campers had previously gotten their jollies by locking themselves in and throwing food through the fence to bears waiting on the outside. That sort of naïve and insensitive entertainment was the likely cause of the problem at Silers.

My boss at that time, Bill Cook, asked me to hike up there and see what was going on. So, bright and early in the morning, I went up to take a look. From the Clingmans Dome parking area, the hike usually took a couple of hours, depending on how many visitors you ran into. Most of it was downhill, which I liked.

I'd just passed the junction of Welch Ridge and the Appalachian Trail when I walked out onto Silers Bald. As the trail opened up on the bald, I saw what looked like items a backpacker might carry while hiking. There were several pieces of female underwear lying on the ground and a backpack that had been ripped open. Nearby was mangled paper from freeze-dried food packs, pots, a flashlight, car keys, a man's billfold, and a man's underwear torn apart.

That couldn't be good.

One of my first thoughts was that a bear had attacked a couple of hikers. My mind raced with frightening scenarios. I stopped and pulled out a few more rounds of twelve-gauge buckshot for the shotgun I was carrying. I'd brought the shotgun to shoot pigs in case I saw any, but now I worried I might have to use it on a homicidal bear.

I'd never had to shoot a charging bear to kill it, but I knew there was first time for everything and wondered if maybe this was it. Watching carefully in all directions, I picked up each item as I found it and stuffed it into the damaged backpack. After I'd retrieved everything, the pack was full and heavy.

The billfold was still intact with credit cards, money, pictures, and other personal items. Whatever happened, it looked like the victims hadn't spent any time trying to save important items like car keys and billfold. I was really concerned about that, but at least I hadn't seen any blood. That was good, I prayed.

It was an eerie parallel to one of the worst signs search and rescue teams come across when they're looking for someone who's become lost in the winter and is freezing to death. When they begin to find pieces of gear and clothing shed along a trail, they know they might be about to discover a dead body because one of the final stages of hypothermia is confusion and an overheating, burning sensation.

The damage to the pack and its contents sure looked like a bear had mauled them, but where were the people? I continued toward the shelter, increasingly worried, wondering if I was getting ready to find someone seriously injured or worse.

When I got to the shelter I found a hysterical man and woman crouching and trembling in the back corner. They were holding on to each other as if they'd just returned from a visit to hell. They were both scared to death.

When they saw me, they acted like they thought I was an angel.

"Oh thank God," they cried, "a ranger. Help us! Please help us!

The man shouted for me to hurry inside the shelter before the bear attacked me, too.

"What bear?" I said.

"Hurry," he said, "get in here!"

So, I went inside the shelter and closed the door. They both leaped up and grabbed me, thanking me for saving them. The lady was holding her throat as if to protect it and touching her chest in a labored effort to breathe. I told them everything was okay now and they were no longer in any danger.

When I finally got them calmed down enough to talk sensibly, they told me they'd hiked up to the bald and seen a bear standing on the side of the trail. They said the bear was going to attack them so they both screamed, threw down their packs, and sprinted down the trail to the shelter.

"Did you try to run the bear off?" I asked.

"No," they said, "the bear was trying to kill us!"

This wasn't the scene that had played out in my mind while I was collecting the torn clothing. I'd imagined a bloodthirsty predatory bear running down two innocent hikers and trying to kill both of them. Now I knew what had actually happened was that some inexperienced hikers had encountered a panhandling bear who'd probably been fed by people before and learned that by approaching them, it might get a free meal.

My perceived danger level from this bear went down significantly. It was serious that a bear would approach anyone for food. But for the couple to not try *at all* to defend themselves and run the bear off to keep it from getting their food wasn't good training for the bear.

The couple was from Ohio and this was their first camping

trip *ever.* They swore to me that if I could get them back to their car, they'd never go backpacking again. *Please keep your promise,* I thought to myself.

I told them I'd walk them back to their vehicle. They kept thanking me and thanking me, over and over. I knew they needed an escort back, but making the return hike with them meant I wouldn't be able to hunt hogs that evening. *Oh well, there's always tomorrow,* I thought.

As they were examining their mauled belongings and rearranging their pack, suddenly a bear weighing about 200 pounds popped around the corner of the shelter and looked in at us. You'd have thought we were being attacked by a pack of lions.

The couple screamed so loud they nearly burst my ear drums. Both of them immediately resumed their cowering in the corner of the shelter where I'd first found them. I bent over to look at them under the bunks. They were holding onto each other yelling, "Shoot him! Shoot him! Shoot him!"

I looked around to see if there was something I was missing. Nope, clearly these were two people who needed to stay on concrete or asphalt or in a high-rise building. I tried again to calm them, but this time there was nothing I could do or say to ease their minds. The bear was standing about fifteen yards away, outside the shelter, calmly looking at the couple, then me.

I wished the bear could talk. I bet it would say something like, *People, what's your problem? Stop screaming, you're hurting my ears! I'm gonna have to move somewhere else like Derrick Knob or Spence Field. The hikers around here are* way *too loud.*

I'd had enough, so I opened the door to the shelter and walked outside. I picked up a rock and charged toward the bear yelling, "Get your butt outta here bear!"

Of course, the bear obliged and took off like a rocket, quickly running out of sight. I told the couple to get up and come with me. We were leaving. As I walked them back to their car, I thought about several things I wanted to say to them but I knew it was a lost cause, so I stayed quiet.

Each time we met other hikers on the trail, the couple said a bear had attacked them. Of course with everyone seeing the ripped up backpack, it was easy to believe their story. The couple scared the fool out of everybody we saw. They were extremely dramatic.

I tried to educate the hikers about what to do if they encountered any bears, but there was no need to worry about any of them having an encounter. Every single person we met on the trail did an about-face and returned at top speed to the Clingmans Dome parking area.

When we finally made it back to the parking lot, I walked the couple to their car and shook their hands and waved as they drove away, heading down the mountain. Then I looked up at the sky and hoped that tomorrow would be a better day . . . and it was.

PEPPER SPRAY

SOME CAMPERS MAY THINK they can stay safe around bears by using pepper spray on their tent or by spraying around their entire campsite.

Bill Stiver is a very dedicated, knowledgeable, and competent wildlife manager who now has my old job of running the wildlife program in the Park. Bill was helping his daughter Baylee with an 8th grade science project to test whether pepper spray would always repel animals or whether it could, under certain circumstances, actually attract critters to objects like tents or backpacks it was sprayed on.

Pepper spray is designed to be used on approaching, or aggressive, or attacking bears during an encounter. But things can work differently if the pepper spray is used ahead of time on inanimate objects.

As a test, Bill and his daughter sprayed pepper spray on a log and set up remote cameras in three separate locations to record what happened. What they saw was that a deer came right up to where they'd used the spray. It smelled and licked the area. A coyote checked it out, too. Then a bear came and investigated every place where the spray had been used and sniffed at it.

So Bill and Baylee proved that if pepper spray is sprayed ahead of time, it can be totally ineffective as a deterrent. In fact, it can be an attractant!

We've learned from a few experiences that, if it's used properly, pepper spray may be even more effective than a gun to stop unwanted bears from approaching. So when anyone is hiking or camping in bear country, it's a good practice to carry along a can of pepper spray. Ninety-nine point nine percent of the time, you won't need it or use it, but when you're out in bear country, you can never say never.

BEAR ATTACK AT CHIMNEYS PICNIC AREA STREAM

WE'VE EXPERIENCED ONLY A HANDFUL of physical altercations between bears and humans that resulted in life-threatening injuries to an innocent Park visitor.

One of them was in 1989 when Phyllis Murphy, a middle-aged lady from Ohio, was attacked by a bear. She and her husband had been regular visitors to the Smokies and had seen bears on several occasions.

Phyllis was walking along the stream at the Chimneys picnic area. She said she bent over beside a boulder to pick up a rock and when she straightened up, a bear stood up at the same time on the other side of the boulder.

She was startled and cried out and turned to run, but she slipped and fell. When she went down, the bear jumped onto her back. Then it bit her in the back, neck, and shoulder. She screamed for help as the attack continued.

Her husband came to her defense, as did other people at the picnic area. Her husband found a big stick and used it to hit the bear hard enough to get the animal off his wife. The bear moved away, but it didn't go far. Witnesses said it went to a nearby garbage can and began to try and get food out of it.

Phyllis was taken to the Emergency Room. She had a broken shoulder blade and slash wounds. Her injuries were serious enough that she was in the hospital for about ten days. She was extremely lucky to be alive. A bite on the neck could've easily paralyzed her, or severed an artery and caused her to bleed to death. This was a close one.

When the incident was reported, we immediately closed the picnic area to visitors. This was the first time I could ever remember closing a front-country campground or picnic area because of a bear incident.

Now we had to try to find the bear responsible for the attack, so we went to the area with spotlights. Chimneys picnic area had always been *the* place for Park visitors to go to see bears and we regularly had to relocate panhandling bears from the area. But we'd never checked to see how many bears were using it at night. We hadn't realized that what happened at night when no visitors were using the area was extremely important.

When we shined our spotlights we were surprised and shocked to find *twelve* bears active there, all at the same time. So there was a serious problem. As we drove around, we saw that every trash can was overfilled and spilling out. Food scraps and garbage were everywhere. It was a much bigger mess than I or anyone else had realized.

This was a whole new level of bear problems. We needed to change our tactics. Something had to be done.

It was a different world back then, before we figured out how to deal effectively with *food-conditioned* bears that had become accustomed to human food instead of their natural diet.

During these early years I was asked by the Tennessee Wildlife Resources Agency to help move some of the panhandling bears out of Gatlinburg. I went to check on a problem reported at the Park Vista Hotel and found *seventeen* bears in the parking lot at the same time. This was the most panhandling bears anyone had ever seen anywhere in one spot at one time.

We compared notes with other parks and I was amazed to learn that in Yosemite National Park, they estimated they had about sixteen bears living in the entire Yosemite Valley. They had 16 to manage and we had 1,600! That showed the magnitude of difference between our problem in the Smokies in comparison to the western Parks. Yosemite has 200,000 more acres of land area, with less than half as many visitors as the Smokies, and a *hundredth* as many bears to manage.

We faced a big challenge in figuring out the best way to manage our bears. Chimneys picnic area, in particular, was a disaster. We moved approximately thirty bears out of there in a three-year period during the late 1980s, but we weren't really solving the problem. We were just dealing with a symptom. The problem was that garbage was being left out overnight and it was attracting bears and causing them to hang around for an easy food supply.

The same year Phyllis Murphy was attacked I caught bears on ninety-eight separate occasions, working nearly every weekend from May through October. Then, once we realized that garbage was causing the problem and took measures to solve that, the number of bears we had to move was drastically reduced.

We were trying a new bear management technique not used by anyone in the world. It focused on changing the behavior of wild bears that were active at night. We learned that this was the only effective time to intervene and be able to successfully change bear behavior once they'd started to visit human areas.

Nowadays, if we have a bear hanging out at night in any area that's regularly used by people, we capture it using a culvert trap and do a biological workup while it's immobilized with drugs. We tag the bear in both ears, tattoo the inside of its lip with a number that matches the ear tag, and pull the first premolar, a very small non-functional tooth.

We can estimate the bear's age by cross-sectioning and staining this tooth, so we can count the rings on it, like the rings on a tree. We also weigh and measure the animal. In some cases, we draw some blood and give the bear any medicines or other care it might need.

What's different about our technique in the Smokies is that we haul the bear right back to where we caught it, and release it. When the bear wakes up from the immobilization drug, he's been asleep and didn't feel anything that happened to him while he was out, just like a person who's been put to sleep during a medical procedure. But he's probably a little sore from where he's had injections and blood drawn and a tooth pulled, so he's rather reluctant to experience that again.

The main point of effectiveness is that the wild animal has been captured and dominated by people. As a cub, the bear was taught by its mom to run from people because humans could hurt bears and, when we reinforce that lesson, the bear realizes that mom was right!

So now most of the bears that have been captured and handled don't want to go around people again and will run from even the smell of humans. Our technique works, at least in our setting. After the bears were captured, handled, and released, most weren't seen in the picnic area again.

It's kind of like going to the dentist or the doctor. It's good for you to go, but when there's some discomfort, we don't really enjoy it. When we put a bear through moderate fear and discomfort, they don't like it either. A bear's memory is unbelievable. They remember the negative experience, just like we do, and it helps teach them not to come into areas that people use.

It's safer for the bear and for Park visitors when the bear is taught not to associate people with an easy and tasty meal, but instead to associate them with a negative experience. When visitors allow bears to get their food, night or day, they teach them bad habits. And that means the wildlife rangers have to intervene to retrain the bears, if we want to save them.

Bears have both an innate and learned fear of humans. When we capture them, we're reminding them of this fear of people and retraining them back to their natural way of thinking after irresponsible tourists have given them dangerous ideas.

It takes time, money, and dedication to retrain wild bears, but that's part of a wildlife ranger's responsibility, and it's worth it. The affected bears may not like it, but it's in their best interest.

DESOLATION CREEK

THEY DIDN'T NAME it Desolation Creek for nothing. If you tried your best to pick a place to go in the Park where no one would ever find you, that would be it.

It just goes to show that sometimes the hardest part of our job is simply getting to and from the jobsite. This was especially the case in the fall of 1979 when the Park Service decided to participate in a brook trout restoration effort with the U.S. Fish and Wildlife Service. In most streams in the Park, the native brook trout, which are actually not *trout* at all, but a type of char, were being forced up to higher elevations and crowded into less attractive habitats by the more aggressive non-native rainbow trout.

Experts decided to begin a reintroduction effort in the extremely remote location of Desolation Creek because it had a waterfall barrier that would keep the rainbow trout from moving back upstream once they were removed.

The plan was that we'd carry in battery-operated backpack shockers to temporarily stun all the fish in a small area of a creek so they could be captured. We'd collect them in buckets and all the rainbow trout and brown trout would be moved downstream below the waterfall, so they couldn't come back and interfere with the less competitive brook trout.

The shockers put out around 700 volts. The jolt from one of them will knock the fool out of you. We wore waders and thick rubber gloves that went all the way to the elbow and used a net to scoop up the fish. If you reached down to pick up a fish barehanded and someone shocked the water while your hand was submerged, the shock would radiate through your whole body. The painful jolt gave you a moment of befuddlement, or *shock*, not knowing if you should run, yell, scream, cuss, or cry.

There was no easy way into Desolation. The traditional route was to take a boat across Fontana Lake to Hazel Creek, then ride an ATV or some sort of vehicle seven miles up Hazel Creek to the Hall Cabin in Bone Valley. A name like Bone Valley should've given me pause, too, but it didn't.

From the Hall Cabin, you had to walk along an old fishermen's manway or in the creek itself to get where we were going. Some of the terrain was so bad, you were on hands and knees crawling under rhododendron, or climbing over it, or stumbling along in the rocky creek bed, getting your boots and feet soaked. I didn't know if that was the best way to get there or not, but it was the traditional route, and the locals usually had the routes worked out as wisely as possible.

But since we were based out of Park Headquarters and heading for the upper area of the creek, we wondered if there might be a better way to get there. I was the crew leader for the Park Conservation Corps crew. Robert Smith, who worked with the U. S. Fish and Wildlife Service, looked at a Park map with me to help plan the trip. Robert suggested it might be better if we drove from Townsend to the end of Tremont Road and hiked the nine miles up to Derrick Knob, hit the Appalachian Trail, traveled west one mile to Sugar Tree Gap, and then *turned left*.

I should've been wary of that vague left turn at the end of his recommended route, but I was too green. The area he was suggesting was very steep and off-trail. To our knowledge, no one had ever gone that way since the Park had been created. I worried we'd encounter what locals call a *slick*, an impenetrable thicket of a rhododendron or laurel, and have to hike a long way to get around it.

We'd be carrying large backpacks which would make it tough to get through thick brush or under low-lying limbs. We were going to have to travel over ten miles before we reached the place where Robert said we should *turn left*. Then we'd have to hike cross-country down the mountain until we hit the creek. "Have you ever hiked that area before?" I asked.

"No," he said, "but I'm fairly sure this route won't be *too* bad. It's shorter anyway."

I knew it was shorter but that didn't mean it would be easier. Robert and I stared at each other for a long moment, until I finally agreed to take his advice. I would hike the crew into the deep wilderness, by a route that none of us had ever attempted.

We set off on our trek. When we got to the cross-country portion of the expedition, our only guidance was to hike downhill into the North Carolina side of the Park. I said a little prayer, asking for God's help in getting us safely to our destination.

Anyone who knew anything about the Park, with its thickets and brambles, and cliffs and briars, would be very reluctant to do this. People can *die* going cross-country. The Park strongly discourages hikers from doing it. Hikers have to have a special permit to camp in cross-country areas, for a good reason. There are so many unknowns. But I was young and naïve and always looking for an adventure.

The going was really slow. We staggered down and down the mountain until we hit a small stream. We followed it, lower and lower, until finally we got all the way downhill and made it to the place we intended to camp. It was pretty unnerving during that hike, going deeper and deeper into the back of beyond, not knowing what we'd find. This was in the days before GPS and cell phones. But God smiled on us and we made it.

In a few days we finished our work, so we packed up as much equipment as we could, and hiked out to the Hall Cabin. We dropped off one load, and then went back for another. We made the round trip again, and dropped off a second load before dark. Everyone was tired, sore, and hungry.

On that second trip people were so exhausted they were stumbling and falling down in the creek on the way back to the Hall Cabin. We should've stopped for the night, but I'd wanted to get all our stuff out of there, knowing we'd probably never be back again. I'd pushed the crew too hard. We'd worked from dawn to dark each day, but they didn't complain.

I was the last person out. I walked behind a girl named Kathy, who was silent the whole way. Her flashlight batteries were so weak she could barely see the ground. I asked her to let me swap batteries with her, but she didn't respond. After a few more minutes of watching her stumble through the brush, I caught up to her, stopped her, switched out the batteries in her flashlight with the ones in mine, and handed her light back to her.

She didn't thank me or say a word. She hadn't wanted to make the second trip that night and I understood. It was a pretty taxing expedition. I sure had all I wanted, and more.

That night some people fired up their stoves to heat water so they could cook a little supper. Others were very quiet and pulled out their sleeping bags and went directly to sleep without eating. We'd brought tents with us, but everyone slept upstairs in the Hall Cabin on old wooden boards instead because it was quicker and easier.

The next morning we hiked out in silence, exhaustion, and misery and were picked up at Fontana Lake. I knew that would be the first and last time I'd ever go to Desolation Creek.

We weren't the only ones who suffered for the brook trout, though. Years later a fisheries crew tried to go to Desolation again, but they missed it and stocked the wrong creek.

Robert Smith, the fellow who'd advised me on the shortcut, later became the Regional Director for the U.S. Fish and Wildlife Service in Hawaii. I've often wondered if, while working in the beauty of Hawaii, Robert ever felt guilty for sending his employees on hikes like the awful one we took to Desolation Creek. My guess, since he stayed in Hawaii, is that he didn't.

THE FASTEST ANIMAL ON EARTH

THE FASTEST ANIMAL ON EARTH is the peregrine falcon. The peregrine, *Falco peregrinus anatum,* is about the same size as a crow, but it can dive at over 200 miles an hour. It can fly vast distances, too. Some peregrines migrate more than 15,000 miles a year, going from Alaska in summer to South America in the winter.

Peregrines had been missing from the Smokies for fifty years. No one was sure why, but they vanished from Tennessee a couple of decades before DDT began causing them to disappear elsewhere. Then, in the 1980s, there was a national effort to restore the falcons. The Park partnered with The Peregrine Fund and my career as a wildlife biologist kicked into high gear.

This was the Park's first attempt to reintroduce a wildlife species to begin the restoration of a native ecosystem in the Smokies. We hoped to bring back the falcons. Unfortunately, by the time the reintroduction effort began, the surviving wild stock had dwindled to such an extent that the program had to rely on breeding different sub-species of peregrines to get a species to restore.

The technique we used to try and reestablish the falcons in the Smokies was to *hack* the birds on high protected cliff ledges. The hacking process involved feeding young birds that couldn't yet fly in a controlled situation, inside a large wooden box with little human contact, until they matured enough to grow flight feathers. You had to get the bird accustomed to the area so they would think of it as their home, or they'd leave and you'd never see them again.

A peregrine nest, called a *scrape* or an *eyrie*, isn't like a regular bird nest. It's just a few rocks and twigs or loose debris on a cliff or a building ledge. Sometimes peregrines will use an old raven nest, and sometimes they'll nest in the hollow cavity of a large tree. But their nesting sites are usually on a rocky cliff, to help avoid predators.

We started our program by taking captive-bred birds to a hack box located high atop a cliff on Greenbrier Pinnacle. In each of the years 1984, 1985, and 1986 a group of young chicks was brought in. We put the little birds in a box and fed them until they grew flight feathers. Then we released them, thirteen birds in all.

Each time we did this the young birds hung around for a while and then flew off, usually heading south. We hoped they'd come back to the Park and breed eventually. Then, in 1987, adult falcons were seen back in the area, so we didn't hack any additional young birds that year because we worried the older birds might kill the younger ones.

For the next ten years, no other falcons were released for fear that the young birds would be killed by returning adults. We had sightings of falcons flying overhead and people heard them screaming, but we never could find a nest or any young, despite searching the cliffs throughout the Park by helicopter.

In early 1997 things changed. We had reports of falcons flying and screaming near Alum Cave on the trail up to Mt. Le Conte. Early each morning we watched carefully to see if the falcons were focusing their activity around any particular location where a nest or scrape might be active.

After a few weeks of watching, one of our talented and devoted volunteers, David Morris, reported that he could see three baby falcon chicks on a scrape located on the side of Little Duck Hawk Ridge, just below a spot called *The Eye of the Needle*. The Eye was an open hole that passed clear through the razor-backed ridge.

It had finally happened. The Park had documented the first successful peregrine falcon nest in Tennessee since 1947. But when they came back, the peregrines didn't come to the place they'd been hacked beginning in 1984. The birds chose a ridge off Alum Cave called Little Duck Hawk Ridge.

Duck hawk is the local dialect name for a peregrine falcon.

There's a Little Duck Hawk Ridge paralleled by Big Duck Hawk Ridge, both near Alum Cave. And Peregrine Peak is the old name for the large mountain where the Alum Cave and the Duck Hawk areas are located.

So all of our science was less wise than the local folks who'd lived in the area before the Park was created and who'd noticed where the birds used to nest. We were pretty embarrassed to have ignored the old names. We should've looked at the map to decide where to re-release the falcons in the first place. Rather than hacking them at Greenbrier Pinnacle, we should've released them at Peregrine Peak or Little or Big Duck Hawk Ridge.

There's not a higher calling or a more satisfying part of a wildlife ranger's job than when a wildlife species is successfully reintroduced into an area where it had been wiped out. There's really no better feeling.

The falcons are still extremely rare in this area. The only known peregrine nests in Tennessee are inside the Great Smoky Mountains National Park and a few other state-protected areas.

One of the places you might see them, though, is at the *Eye of the Needle,* the distinctive rock formation with a hole all the way through a cliff, viewable from Inspiration Point off the Alum Cave Trail. Late winter and early spring, or August through September, are the most likely times to see them. To locate their nests, look for the *whitewash* covering the cliff where their bird droppings fall.

It's wonderful to see the young falcons practice-diving off a cliff.

Adult peregrines eat medium size birds. They feed their chicks with doves, cardinals, and blue jays, and other similar-size birds. When they hunt, they circle high in the air watching for prey to fly below them. Once they've locked in on a particular bird, they engage in a *stoop* to attack their prey.

The stoop is amazing. The birds pull in their wings, tail, and feet, and dive in a high-speed freefall. One peregrine was clocked at 242 miles an hour. They hit their prey with closed talons to stun it or break its back and kill it. Then they return to pick it up in mid-air or, if it's too heavy, they let it fall to the ground.

A few years after the falcons returned to the Smokies, one of our birds paired up with a bird hacked in Shenandoah and together they moved to Pennsylvania! The pair nested on a skyscraper in downtown Pittsburgh where they feasted on the relatively naïve pigeons. For peregrines, life in the big city, dining on the city birds was like eating out every night.

HONEYMOON FROM HELL

PEREGRINE FALCONS SCREAM when they dive. People who hear the scream say it's quite memorable. That's why a bird expert would want to record it. We're often asked for permits to make audio recordings in the Park. One of the fellows we gave several permits to is Mark Dunaway, a bird biologist and a wilderness audio expert.

Mark specializes in recording the sounds of critters in their natural habitat. When he was earning his Masters Degree in Biology, he worked for three years to make a set of audio CDs called *Bird Songs of the Smokies*. He made more than fifty visits to the Park and worked long hours to get recordings of bird calls from sixty-seven different species.

It wasn't an easy job. The hardest part was getting recordings without any background noise. Mark said it was especially difficult to get clean recordings of the falcons. "There's nearly always something making an interfering racket," he said, "usually tourists."

"You can't get to the place where the peregrines are before daylight," he said, "because it's two miles up a trail. It's between eight and ten in the morning before you can get there, and by that time people are already coming down from spending the night at the Lodge up on Mt. Le Conte.

"When they see me with all my equipment, it's obvious what I'm doing, but most of them have never seen a peregrine falcon before, so when they do they keep saying, 'Wow!' I have to ask them repeatedly to be quiet so I can get a usable recording."

In the same way wildlife rangers wear camouflage when we need to be inconspicuous, Mark wears a ghilley suit when he stalks birds. His suit is an elaborate camouflage coverall with individual leaves sewn onto it like the ones snipers use. He even has leaves sewn on his headphones. So, when Mark is in his camo, sitting still in the woods, he can be very hard to see.

The best times to record bird sounds are at dawn and dusk, so Mark is usually hiking to and from his work locations in the dark. This doesn't bother him though, because he happens to be blind. His brother, Dustin, or his wife, Marci, take him to wherever he needs to go, help him get settled comfortably, then leave him alone for however long he wants to work.

Mark's unselfconscious appearance has created some unique encounters with Park visitors. I always enjoy hearing about them because it's comforting to know that wildlife rangers aren't the only ones who get into awkward situations.

We know Mark not only on account of the permits he has to get. We're also very familiar with him because of all the reports we get from tourists about sightings of a brazen poacher, a not so sneaky terrorist, Bigfoot, or *Swamp Thing*.

Mark's costume has inadvertently led him to become something of an expert in recording screams. He's recorded all kinds—some on purpose and some as accidents. The ones he records on purpose are from birds, like falcons. The ones he's gotten by accident are from people. He has a large catalog of screams emanating from deep inside the Park, from birds, rangers, tourists, and even himself.

He swears he doesn't record what he refers to as *non-bird sounds* on purpose. He says these human screams always happen unexpectedly. But, I can tell you, they happen a lot when Mark's around.

One of the funniest recordings was made during an evening when he was sitting on a stump alongside a trail in Cades Cove. He'd been sitting there for a long time, hoping to record American Woodcock sounds, when a newlywed couple came strolling along the path, hand in hand, enjoying the sunset. Mark says he always feels awkward when he realizes people are nearby who don't see him, but he says it's a tough call deciding whether to say anything or not, and then picking just the right moment to say it.

On this occasion, the young couple was obviously enjoying what they thought was a private, romantic walk, so he hesitated to announce his presence. Then, when they were about twenty-five yards away he heard the man say in a relaxed, dreamy tone of voice, "That looks almost like a man sitting there on that stump."

Mark thought it best to speak up, so he said, "It *is* a man."

The young husband was so shocked at being spoken to by what looked like a talking shrub, he screamed.

"It was a long, agonized, blood-curdling shriek," said Mark. "It went on and on. His wife wasn't scared at all, but the guy was hysterical. My own wife, Marci, heard the scream two hundred yards away and she was sitting inside a car with the windows rolled up, studying for her doctorate in psychology.

"She called me on the walkie-talkie to make sure I was okay. I tried to explain that it wasn't me making all the noise. At the same time I was also trying to tell the man who I was, but I don't think he was listening. He couldn't stop screaming.

"After something like that, I might as well pack up," Mark said. "That racket scared off every bird for miles. I've always wondered how their marriage worked out. I'm afraid a guy screaming like a little girl in front of the new missus wasn't an ideal start for a lifetime of wedded bliss.

"I accidentally gave those people a *Honeymoon from Hell*," he said, shaking his head, "and I've got it on tape."

BEARS IN THE SHADOWS

WILD HOG HUNTING, government-style, has evolved a lot over the years. We used to hunt wild hogs by having someone go along with the hunter and stand behind them shining a light on the pesky rooters. Then we hunted alone, lugging our own cumbersome spotlight, and after that we progressed to using a more portable light.

Nowadays, thanks to a kind donor, we have state-of-the-art night vision goggles. And also thanks to that same generous supporter and some special government monies, we now have several sound-suppressed rifles.

Suppressors help us keep the noise down. If the bullet itself is moving faster than the speed of sound, if it's breaking the sound barrier, you'll still hear the crack. But muffling the racket helps the hunters be more effective in reducing the number of wild hogs that are doing so much damage to the Park.

A big pig in the Smokies these days is 125-150 pounds. They stay extremely fit and trim by running up and down the hills. The wild hogs in the Smokies behave like *Rooshins*, or purebred Russian boars, but the shape of their bodies looks more like feral pigs.

Wild hogs root around because they're looking for tubers, earthworms, and acorns. They also need to eat dirt to get enough iron in their diet. In addition, they wallow in the mud to try to rid themselves of external parasites. Hogs prefer to be nocturnal because there's less disturbance from people at night. There's security in darkness. And since hogs don't sweat, going out mainly at night helps them stay cool and regulate their temperature.

For the same reason, hogs like to go up into the higher altitudes of the Park when it begins to warm up. We learned this when we put radio collars on some pigs in the 1970s and saw how they tended to migrate as the seasons changed.

Just like people, wild animals prefer to travel on a trail if possible, rather than wading through the undergrowth. In the late spring and summer months, hogs run along the Appalachian Trail and the high ridges, eating one of the Park's famous flowering plants, Spring beauties. So we search along the trail in order to get to the areas where the hogs are feeding and also to be able to stalk the animals as quietly as possible.

We wear camouflage clothing to hunt in and sometimes we use laser aiming devices, too. We have several bits of technology that help give us the upper hand, but we need it because we're hunting one of the smartest and toughest wild animals to find and eliminate.

All sorts of things happen when we're out alone, in the dark, hunting hogs. One of the strangest is being followed by bears night after night. It's a worrisome experience and it's happened to three different hog hunters.

First it happened to Ranger Tim Francis between Molly's Ridge and Gregory Bald. Tim expressed his concern to me one Friday when he arrived at Headquarters after a week-long hunting trip.

One night while hiking on the Appalachian Trail near Doe Knob he heard something behind him. He turned around, shined his spotlight, and saw a fairly large bear looking back at him.

Tim had been hearing something moving along behind him for a mile or so, but never could see what it was. Now he knew. A bear was following him.

"The bear learned to stay about thirty or forty yards behind me," Tim said.

The bear apparently had figured out that Tim resulted in big fat hog carcasses lying along the ridge, and was patiently following him, hoping for a free dinner. Bears are extremely smart. They learn quickly what a rifle shot sounds like, and they learn what it means.

That bear had learned that a gunshot in a certain area often resulted in an easy meal. We knew that for many years, a gunshot in Alaska has been like ringing a dinner bell for the grizzlies, but we hadn't realized the same thing was also becoming true with black bears in the Smokies.

Being followed by a bear in daylight would be a serious concern, too, because there's always the concern that the bear might be predatory. But bears are generally nocturnal, so at night, although it's creepy, the situation indicated the bear was simply looking for an easy meal, a hog carcass.

Terry Esker, a wildlife technician originally from Illinois, was hunting one night and was about six miles from the *Shoat*, a Dodge pickup truck. He'd shot a pig and was bent over it attempting to determine its age from tooth eruption and tooth wear when he heard a noise on the hillside above him. He turned his spotlight and saw a very large bear standing there looking down at him.

The bear began to approach Terry and was blowing, moaning, and popping his jaws. Then, without warning, he came bouncing down the steep hill like a huge baboon, huffing and grunting each time he hit the ground. Terry realized that the bear wanted to claim the hog, so he backed away from the pile of bacon and let the bear have it.

When Terry had moved only a few yards away, the bear raced in and grabbed the pig in his jaws and took off with it. The bear carried a 200-pound hog by the back of the neck like it was an empty paper bag. Terry, who was in a state of shock, made his way back up to the Appalachian Trail to get away from the bear and continue his search for hogs.

When he arrived back at Headquarters Terry told me what had happened and said, "Sorry I wasn't able to get the age of the pig."

"No problem," I said. "I would've done the same thing, probably even quicker."

We knew hog carcasses disappeared in the Park overnight, but it was an unnerving experience to be right there when it happened.

Ranger Dan Nolfi had a similar experience between Molly's Ridge and Russell Field. He'd shot a hog beside the trail and was dragging the carcass off into the shrubbery when he heard something coming through the brush from below him. Thinking it was another hog, he went back into hog-hunting mode.

He waited with his gun raised and aimed in the direction of the approaching sound. Just as he was ready to shoot what he thought was a hog, a large bear popped out of the underbrush and stared at him and the dead pig.

After a brief staring match, the bear charged toward the hog carcass and Dan went into reverse gear. The bear snatched the hog, turned, and ran down the mountain as if carrying his lunchbox to school.

Dan was stunned by the boldness of the bear. Clearly a hungry bear will do whatever it has to do to find food. It's a basic survival instinct that's necessary to live another day in the mountains.

All three situations occurred at night, at high elevation, along the western section of the Appalachian Trail as it passes through the Park. In each case, the hunters knew they were being followed systematically because they could hear the bear moving through the woods. And in each case the bear was on the scene almost immediately after the shot was fired.

I'm not sure how a bear would act if it showed up expecting to find something to eat and the hunter's shot had missed its mark. I can't imagine the bear would be pleased.

MY WORST DAY IN THE GREAT SMOKY MOUNTAINS NATIONAL PARK

MY WORST DAY at work, my worst memory of thirty-two years in the Park, was May 21, 2000. That was the day Glenda Ann Bradley died.

In the entire seventy-five-year history of the Park there's been only *one* known fatality from a bear attack. It was Glenda Bradley, a fifty year old school teacher who taught at Jones Cove Elementary near Cosby, Tennessee. Cosby is a very rural area adjacent to the Park.

Glenda was an experienced hiker who went into the Park with her ex-husband, Ralph Hill. They set off walking along the Little River Trail in Elkmont at about noon. Ralph planned to walk along the river and fish. Glenda brought a book she intended to sit and read. Ralph started fishing and Glenda hiked farther up the trail to a footbridge that crossed the river near the intersection of Little River Trail and Goshen Prong Trail.

She sat down beside the river, near the trail, on a stump she called *The Octopus*. The couple had agreed that she'd stay there until Ralph fished up the river to meet her and then they'd hike out together. This location was about three and a half miles into the backcountry.

After an hour, it started to rain. Ralph fished up to the spot where Glenda normally sat, but when he got there, she was gone. He hiked up Goshen Prong Trail looking for her. Soon, he met up with a couple of hikers and asked them if they'd seen her. They hadn't. Both Ralph and the two hikers walked back to the area near the river where Glenda was supposed to be waiting.

In an interview with Ralph following the incident, he told me that he and the others yelled for Glenda, calling her name, but heard no response. Then they widened their search off-trail and soon came upon two bears, a mother and a yearling. On closer inspection, Ralph could see the adult bear was standing over something. When he got even closer, he realized the bear was standing over Glenda.

He and the two hikers approached the spot where Glenda lay, yelling at the bears and throwing sticks and rocks at them, trying desperately to scare them away, but the mother bear was extremely possessive of Glenda's body. Ralph and the others weren't able to make the bears leave, so he went for help. Ralph told me later that he tried hard to make them go away, but they just wouldn't leave. He kept saying, "I tried, I tried."

At about 5 p.m. he encountered another hiker and explained what had happened and asked the fellow to go to Elkmont Campground and ask the rangers there for help. The hiker did as Ralph asked.

Rangers arrived on the scene at 6:05 p.m. The two bears had been feeding on her body. The mother bear was still extremely aggressive toward anyone who approached, and viciously defended the body and her position by charging the rangers several times, even when they grouped together and charged the bears.

Then Ranger Jerry Grubb arrived at the scene with Chip Nelson and they shot and killed the five year old, 111-pound adult female bear and her forty-pound female yearling.

The autopsy of Glenda Bradley showed that she died of blood loss from the injuries inflicted by the bears. Her death was ruled an accident. The behavior of the bears was determined to be predatory in nature.

Later that evening, I hauled the carcasses of both bears to the University of Tennessee College of Veterinary Medicine and participated in the necropsies alongside the vet school staff. The examinations of both bears showed there was little or no food in their stomachs prior to their attack on Glenda.

Neither bear was in good shape. Both had very little body fat. But there was nothing obviously wrong with either of them, other than the appearance that they'd been extremely hungry. The mother bear was wearing ear tags. She'd been tagged earlier by the University of Tennessee as part of their black bear research program.

She was first captured and radio-collared in August of 1998. She was then recaptured in her den the following winter in February of 1999 and observed to have had three baby cubs with her in her den. During this visit, the University bear researchers placed an orphaned male cub from Appalachian Bear Rescue in with the group, giving the mother bear a total of four cubs.

At some point after that the mother bear lost her collar. It might've slipped off due to weight loss. During the course of fifteen months she lost two of her own cubs and the ABR cub. We don't know what happened to them. They could've starved, or been in accidents, or been killed by male bears. But neither the mother bear nor the surviving yearling had any history of causing problems with people or otherwise.

Glenda's daypack had food in it, but it hadn't been disturbed by the bears. Many people wondered why the bears didn't go for the food in her pack. The fact that the bears weren't interested in the food in Glenda's backpack, the time of the year, the persistence of the attack, the bears' consumption of human tissue, and the lack of any prior history of problems with the bears led us to believe this attack was truly predatory.

We don't know all the details about what really happened. We will *never* know everything that happened before the attack. We do know that during a black bear attack, playing dead usually doesn't work. Playing dead is the recommended strategy in the event of a grizzly bear attack, but there are no grizzly bears in the Great Smoky Mountains National Park.

There were indications that Glenda may have run from the bears. Investigators on the scene tracked the bear that killed her through the vegetation and could see Glenda's tracks and the bear's tracks joining near the area where her body was located.

Glenda had also taken two photos of the bear with her camera prior to the attack. The pictures on her camera show that Glenda and the bears were on opposite sides of the footbridge that crossed Little River. Her backpack was found in the vegetation near the footbridge. There was a candy bar and a candy bar wrapper in it, but the bears went right past the food and went for her.

Glenda's death was a terrible tragedy. Fortunately for other Park visitors, an event like this is *extremely* rare. In 2000, Glenda Bradley was the only known victim of a fatal black bear attack in the Great Smoky Mountains National Park, in any other U.S. National Park, or in the Southeastern United States.

During all the years I worked with bears and other wildlife in the Park, I felt responsible for the animals, no matter what they did, good or bad. The feeling of responsibility came with the territory, I guess. I wanted everyone to be able to enjoy God's creation and His creatures. We are placed on this earth as stewards over the animals and their habitat. But sometimes bad things happen that we can't prevent or change, no matter how much we wished we could.

Although I'm retired from the Park now, I continue to teach workshops to help educate bear managers about how to do the best possible job to protect people and manage wildlife. It's a big responsibility and one they should take very seriously.

I kept the memorial card from Glenda's funeral on the wall of my office for the remainder of the time I worked at the Park, eleven more years. I kept it as a constant reminder to do absolutely everything in my power to protect visitors and to manage bears professionally and responsibly.

It's a difficult balancing act. When I left my office at Headquarters for the last time in January of 2011, I brought the memorial card home with me. It stays on the desk in my home office to remind me of Glenda and that what happened on May 21, 2000. Every time I think of Glenda and the incident, I still get a lump in my throat. Although I didn't know her before the attack, I was told she was a great school teacher and a wonderful person. I wish I could've been there that Sunday afternoon to help her. To this day, her death sticks in my mind and I know it always will.

TOYING WITH BEARS

LAUREL FALLS TRAIL is the most heavily used trail in the Park. It's common to have over 1,000 hikers a day use the 1.3 mile trail from the parking area to the falls. Thousands of hikers bring in a lot of food and leave a lot of garbage behind. The smell of the food attracts bears.

This is the main reason we have a lot of bear problems along the Laurel Falls Trail. Also, this area is relatively close to Gatlinburg and it's possible that food-conditioned bears from Gatlinburg make visits here as well. All in all, Laurel Falls is a common site for bear-people encounters, some good and some bad.

In May of 2010 a bad encounter occurred there between a tourist and a bear. A young sixty-pound female bear had been seen in the area around Laurel Falls for several days. Just before the incident occurred, the bear was seen walking downstream from the top of Laurel Falls. There were several hikers standing below the Falls taking pictures and resting. The bear walked toward the people and none of them attempted to chase it away.

The bear continued to meander through the area while people blithely took pictures with little regard for the fact that only a few feet away was a wild animal that could severely injure them. Other visitors remained sitting on a wooden bench at the base of the Falls while the bear walked underneath it. One of these people had an umbrella and he allowed the bear to chew on the end of it while he held the umbrella in his hand.

The naïveté and ignorance of some Park visitors is worrisome and dangerous, and it's a wonder bears don't hurt visitors more often than they do. Many, many people are simply clueless about how to behave properly in bear country.

While the bear and tourists continued to interact, there was a man from Connecticut, Sean Konover, who was downstream from the falls, watching the fiasco unfold. He decided to walk back up to the main trail. When he reached the trail, he turned toward the falls because this was the only way to get back to the parking lot and his vehicle.

He saw the bear coming toward him on the trail. Sean said he moved to the left of the trail and stood against a rock wall hoping the bear would move on past him. However, when the bear got close to him, he took a couple of pictures of it. Then the bear turned toward him, and bit him on the foot.

Sean yelled and scared the bear away. It moved farther up along the trail. Sean took another photo of the bear after it bit him.

When the incident was reported, I sent a couple of the wildlife guys up to the area to look for the bear. It was late in the evening by the time our guys arrived at the falls and there was no sign of the bear. The next day, I sent Rick Varner and an intern to patrol the site.

While Rick was there, a bear appeared that was the same size as the one we were looking for. Rick darted it, hauled it down the trail on a wheeled litter, and transported it back to the Wildlife Building. We held the bear for about a week and continued to monitor the area around the Laurel Falls Trail in case another bear showed up, but no other bears were seen.

Normally we euthanize bears that break into cars, tents, or homes; or bears that are extremely aggressive toward people or injure anyone. That has historically meant about one or two bears a year. We can't allow bears with dangerous, or potentially dangerous, behaviors to roam around loose among people and continue to hurt people, or worse.

After a bear has bitten someone, even a small bite, the next time the animal behaves badly, it might attack a child and severely injure or kill them. A bear that's even as small as sixty pounds can seriously harm or kill someone.

When bears aim to kill something, they don't play games. Their sharp claws and large teeth are like a dozen pairs of scissors coming at you. Bears are potentially dangerous. They play for keeps! So, we ultimately decided to euthanize the bear captured at Laurel Falls. When we put this bear or any other wild animal down, we act in accordance with methods approved by the American Veterinary Medical Association in their Guidelines for the Euthanasia of Animals.

The injury to Sean's foot was relatively minor, a couple of small puncture wounds, but it could've been much worse. It didn't require treatment at a hospital. He initially was cited for approaching a bear too closely, but once a thorough investigation was completed, the charge was dismissed.

In an interview with Sean, he told me he didn't approach the bear, but rather the bear approached him before it bit him. He admitted that he should've yelled and tried to scare the bear away, but he didn't and that was not a good choice on his part.

Soon after the bear was captured, a Facebook page was created, naming the misbehaving bear *Laurel*. It garnered more than 7,000 fans who hoped to prevent the Park from euthanizing the bear.

Social pressure or emotion, however, isn't a good way to manage a bear population. When 1,600 bears and nine million people, many of whom are naïve about wildlife, are using the same area, bad things sometimes happen.

Several people complained that Laurel wasn't at fault and said that the incident had been caused by the person who was bitten. They suggested in all seriousness that we shoot and kill the person who was bitten. That obviously wasn't a reasonable or wise solution. At times, some people seem to value animals such as bears more than humans. I don't.

161

When a bear has so little fear of humans as to come into physical contact with a person and bite them, we think the best thing to do, to protect people and all the other bears, is to put the offending bear down. This prevents that bear from teaching any other bears to do the same thing, and it prevents the bear from passing along aggressive tendencies to their offspring. This is the best way we know to protect the integrity of the Smokies wild bear population.

I personally euthanized Laurel the Bear by lethal injection. The process was quick and painless to her. I wasn't proud of it and I hoped I'd never have to put another bear down again.

I love wildlife. I appreciate and respect wild animals. I've devoted my entire professional life to caring for them. Most of my job as a wildlife ranger was rewarding and enjoyable. This part of it wasn't, and I hated it.

THE PARK'S MOST FAMOUS BEAR

THE MOST FAMOUS BEAR in the history of the Great Smoky Mountains National Park was Bear #75.

In July of 1988, Bear #75 ripped the side out of the historic John P. Cable Mill in Cades Cove so he could get in and eat the beef fat, or tallow, from the stone wheel that ground corn to make cornmeal. He was also seen rummaging through garbage from overfilled containers at the Mill and at the nearby Abrams Falls Trailhead.

When the rangers in Cades Cove went to deal with him they noticed he had little fear of people. He moved through crowds of tourists carefully, neither cowering nor aggressive. This wasn't normal, and it wasn't a good situation. Bear #75 was a large handsome fellow. The locals had even named him, they called him Brutus. He was a superb specimen. If a bear population had a king, it would've been Brutus.

Brutus had once been totally afraid of people but, because of the availability of garbage, he was changing, and not for the better. He was losing his fear of people. This is one of the fundamental behaviors necessary for bears and other wildlife to survive in the wild. People are the only predator of black bears and losing their fear of us only jeopardizes their survival.

Wild bears have both a natural and a genetically-based fear of humans and the scent associated with them. Brutus had somehow managed to overcome this. Probably he'd been trained by tourists who gradually enticed him closer and closer, first by leaving garbage where he could find it during the night, then by baiting him with food during the day, so they could take photos of the majestic bear. Unfortunately, he became comfortable around crowds.

A wild bear in close proximity with people is definitely dangerous for the people and it's not good for the bear's health either. We know garbage is bad for bears. Human food can cause tooth decay in bears the same way it does in people. Studies have shown that unnatural tooth decay occurs in raccoons that get hooked on garbage.

Research has also shown that some bears that get food-conditioned on garbage go through a physiological change and may never be able to feed naturally as a wild bear again. Either way, we know that **GARBAGE KILLS BEARS**. We needed to do our best to prevent garbage from becoming a primary source of food for Brutus.

Our first line of attack was to eliminate all the food and garbage from around the Mill and Cades Cove Visitor Center. We tried, but two million people are just too many for us to control both day and night. We then tried various techniques to scare Brutus away, but with no luck. He had already stopped being nocturnal and was now active around people during the day, so keeping food and garbage away from him was impossible.

Brutus wasn't a mean bear. We didn't want to have to kill him, so we decided to relocate him to an area with fewer people and much less available human food.

Cades Cove Rangers trapped Brutus and brought him to Park Headquarters. I drugged him so we could tag, tattoo, and collect some information from him. While he was asleep, I lifted up one of his front legs and saw that he had a large open wound in his armpit. It was about three or four inches in diameter and needed to be cleaned and stitched up before we released him.

I took him to the University of Tennessee Veterinary Hospital for treatment. After they cared for him, he was again ready to trek up and down the Smoky Mountains. We relocated Brutus to Cataloochee on the North Carolina side of the mountains. This was as far away as we could take him and yet still remain within the boundary of the Park.

Ten days later I was sitting in my office when a call came in around noon reporting that a big bear was walking down the middle of Hwy. 441 just above Park Headquarters. A bear in this area would definitely cause a sensation. He ambled down the middle of the main highway through the Park, passed by Park Headquarters, then walked through the employee housing area, making his way to the Flats on Little River Road just above Headquarters.

Dispatch called with the location of the bear and said a traffic jam was being caused by people looking at him. I loaded my capture equipment into the *Boar* truck and drove up the road. Soon I located the mass of people and cars surrounding the big bear. He was sitting on the side of the road calmly, as if waiting for someone to throw him a snack.

Well, I was going to throw him something, but it wasn't going to be food. Instead I used a dart full of immobilization drugs. The dart hit its mark and within minutes I was able to pull the truck up next to the bear.

At first I assumed it was a garbage bear that had wandered over from the Gatlinburg area because there were so many of them over there. But when I looked down and noticed the bear was tagged, I wondered who this bear was and where he'd come from.

When I reached down and grabbed his front leg to turn him over, I noticed a wound and stitches on the inside of his leg. That injury sure looked familiar. I leaned over and grabbed the ear tag to take a look and was shocked to see #75. It was Brutus. Apparently he wasn't satisfied with Cataloochee and was making his way back to Cades Cove. Traveling by Headquarters made it seem like he wanted to stop by to visit me on his way. If that was his intention, I'm not sure the visit turned out as he'd hoped.

Knowing there was nowhere else in the Park that I could relocate him, I called Tennessee Wildlife Resources Agency and asked if I could take him south to the Ocoee Wildlife Management Area, a bear sanctuary east of Chattanooga, Tennessee that's near the Tennessee-Georgia state line. By air, it was nearly sixty miles from Cades Cove. It's much farther on the ground, of course.

I thought this was the last time Brutus and I would ever see each other. Boy, was I wrong. Three and a half weeks after his release he was captured in Cades Cove, again, and taken back to Cataloochee, North Carolina, again. I was running out of places to take him and was getting a little frustrated.

I'm not sure where Brutus slept that winter, but the next summer he showed up back in Cades Cove for a third time and was relocated, again, to Ocoee. He could've stayed there. I thought he might make a wrong turn coming back to Cades Cove, but he didn't.

A month later, after his trip to Ocoee, Brutus was back in Cades Cove for the fourth time. This time he was taken over 130 miles away to Sullivan County, Tennessee, fairly close to the Virginia state line.

Two weeks later he was captured by officers of the Tennessee Wildlife Resources Agency in Johnson City, Tennessee as he walked through the parking lot of the Veterans Administration hospital. They called me and wanted to know his history. His rap sheet was already fairly long, and it was getting longer.

The wildlife people in Johnson City were shocked that he'd traveled so far in an effort to get back to his home in Cades Cove. They said they were going to release him in Carter County, a remote area in northeastern Tennessee.

The next spring, Brutus returned to Cades Cove for the fifth time. He was an amazing navigator and obviously had a strong attachment to his home in the cove. I don't know how he was able to do what he did. It was as if Brutus had his own built-in GPS unit.

How could this or any other bear travel such rugged territory, swimming rivers and lakes, crossing busy highways, parking lots, and subdivisions without getting killed? He was living on the edge for sure.

At this point, a long-range relocation was the only thing that might work to keep Brutus away from Cades Cove where he caused problems. I thought I'd moved him far enough away when I sent him to North Carolina and then almost to the Virginia and Georgia state lines, but he proved me wrong every time.

The very last option would be to put him down. But no one, especially me, wanted to do that. I was getting calls from people asking what I was going to do with him. Brutus had become a celebrity in the bear world. He'd made a connection with a lot of people. I was worried about his fate.

I sat in my office looking at a Tennessee map trying to figure out somewhere to release him. I looked toward the south, to Georgia. There was too much development there. It stretched all the way to Atlanta, so that wasn't a good option.

I looked toward the north, to the line of Appalachian Mountains bordered by the Shenandoah Valley. The north looked much better. I wondered if this might be a viable possibility.

A good longtime friend of mine, Bob Duncan, was the Chief of Wildlife for the Virginia Department of Game and Inland Fisheries, so I thought, *What the heck*. I decided to give him a call. All he could say was, *No!* It was worth a shot.

In a few minutes, I had Bob on the line and described my predicament. I gave him Brutus's history and explained that he wasn't a bad bear, but was food-conditioned in Cades Cove. I told Bob that Brutus wasn't aggressive or dangerous and had never hurt anyone. He was just a bear who had learned how to get food from people.

I explained that Brutus never got into any trouble in any of the places we released him and never caused any problems on his way back to Cades Cove. But, when he got home, he picked up his old habits and caused a sensation among visitors and that created a potentially dangerous situation in the Park.

I assured Bob that if Brutus caused any problems, I'd come get him. That sealed the deal. Bob reluctantly gave me the go-ahead to move the bear. I thanked Bob sincerely and told him that I owed him one, or rather Brutus owed him one.

This time I hauled Brutus 400 air miles from Cades Cove to Virginia's state bear catcher, Jerry Blank, who lived in Harrisonburg. Jerry had worked with the bear program for the Virginia Department of Game and Inland Fisheries for his entire career. He'd captured and successfully relocated literally *hundreds* of bears, primarily ones that were damaging farmers' cornfields.

Jerry knew all about problem bears. When he relocated a bear, he usually drove it to the George Washington National Forest and released it on an old logging road near the Virginia-West Virginia state line. Would this be Brutus' last release? I thought it would be, but I found out differently.

This time, before we released Brutus, we put a radio collar on him so we could track him.

Jerry took Brutus to his best release spot and let the bear out of the cage and watched to see what would happen. Jerry told me that of all the hundreds of bears he'd released at this same spot, every single one of them had jumped out of the cage as soon as the door was opened and then headed north until they ran out of sight.

He figured this bear would do the same thing. But he didn't.

As Jerry climbed on top of the bear transfer box, Brutus was slapping the cage letting Jerry know that he wasn't happy and that he wanted out. Jerry carefully pulled the cage door open, assuming

Brutus would do the same thing that every single one of the other bears had done in the past. But Brutus was not just *any* bear. There was something unique about him. He had a strong will and keen desire to get back to Cades Cove, his home.

When the door was opened, he jumped to the ground, but he ran only a short distance, then stopped, sniffed the air, and started bobbing his head as he looked around. Then he changed direction, turning south, heading back toward Tennessee.

Brutus gave Jerry and his truck a wide berth as he circled around them, headed south, starting his long journey back home. This was especially amazing because Brutus was drugged and had been sound asleep during the entire six-hour trip from Cades Cove to Virginia.

How was he able to know which way to go?

Jerry was absolutely stunned. He couldn't believe it. No other bear had ever done this. What was going on? As the bear loped off heading south, Jerry ran after him trying to steer him back to the north, but no luck. Brutus was going home!

We tracked Brutus by means of his radio collar. He managed to travel south an average of ten to twelve miles every night. In a few weeks, he was caught in Pearisburg, Virginia, just west of Blacksburg, and taken back north again, even farther than he'd been taken the first time. And then, again, every night we tracked him moving ten to twelve miles south.

A few days later he was spotted walking through a residential area in the town of Roanoke, Virginia. The Roanoke Police Department responded to the calls to capture and move the bear out of town. Unfortunately, though, the drug they used to immobilize Brutus didn't knock him out completely.

This meant the police didn't dare put their hands on him to load him into a vehicle for his ride out of town. He had to be lassoed with a rope and pulled into the back of a police van instead. I'm sure that was a sight to see. I wouldn't have wanted to be on the other end of that rope, though, especially pulling a bear into a closed space with me.

During the brief amateur rodeo and struggle with Brutus, his radio collar was accidentally pulled off and it couldn't be put back on because the bear was now wide awake. Without the right drugs to knock him out completely, there was no way to replace the collar. And, honestly, after this ordeal, putting a radio collar back on the bear was probably the last thing on the policemen's minds. So, we lost the ability to know Brutus's exact whereabouts.

Were we through with Brutus? Would we ever hear from him again?

A month later officials of the Tennessee Wildlife Resources Agency got a call saying a big bear was seen walking through the grounds of the Veterans Administration hospital in Johnson City, Tennessee. The wildlife officers darted the bear and when they rolled him over they were shocked to see the #75 tag in his ear. They couldn't believe their eyes. This was the same bear and in the same location where they'd captured him a year before, but a lot had happened to Brutus since then.

For a bear that loved human food from Cades Cove so much, it was interesting to note that he apparently ate only wild foods during his long and frequent travels back to the cove. On this trip through Johnson City, he took a route that happened to pass by a Kentucky Fried Chicken, but despite the tempting odors he didn't try to go inside or sneak through the drive-thru. His photo was snapped as he walked past the front of the restaurant and it ran in the local newspaper.

By this time, Brutus was a genuine celebrity. I know a bunch of people were pulling for him to make it back to Cades Cove. I may have been one of them.

The capture in Johnson City at the Veteran's Hospital parking lot was Brutus's *tenth* live capture, and it turned out to be his last one. Officers of the Tennessee Wildlife Resources Agency hauled him to nearby Carter County and released him there again.

Brutus made his way to Unicoi County, Tennessee where three days later, while eating blackberries near a residential area, he was shot and killed by a poacher for no apparent reason. There was a sizable reward for the arrest and conviction of the poacher, but no one was ever caught.

Brutus was dead.

A necropsy was performed and we discovered that, although Brutus had encountered many people and had never hurt any of them, some of the people he'd been around weren't very kind to him. We learned that he had a variety of types of bullets and shot in him. He had small bird shot in his hip, a .22 caliber bullet in his shoulder, and buckshot in his neck. It was the buckshot in his neck that was the cause of his death.

Brutus was relocated one last time. This time to a site where he was buried by the wildlife workers who'd worked so hard to keep him alive.

In less than two years, Brutus had been captured ten times. He'd traveled more than 1,500 air miles on his own four legs. Every inch of it had been made in a simple effort to go home.

At the start of all this, Brutus did nothing wrong. Not really. He simply ate the food people gave him, or ate what they left out so he could find it. As a result, he lost his fear of people. That caused his ultimate downfall. If Brutus had never been able to get into garbage, never gotten a handout from anyone, he wouldn't have been a problem, and wouldn't have had to die so young.

It says a lot about black bears and about Brutus that even with hundreds of encounters with people, he never hurt a single person. But despite his gentle nature, he died because of the ignorance, self-ishness, and laziness of some of the visitors to Cades Cove. Brutus died because people came to his home and taught him fatal habits that would never have occurred to him if they had only been a little more responsible.

The tourists who failed to keep their food and garbage away from Brutus went back home happy with their photos and their stories, but what they did to the poor bear baited him past the point of no return. For a few minutes of thrill-seeking, or a few mediocre photos that would languish forgotten in dusty photo albums, Brutus died.

Please remember Brutus when you visit the Park. Remember him and tidy up your campsite or picnic table before you leave the area. There's a good reason to leave a clean site—*Garbage Kills Bears*.

In the case of Brutus, although he died from being shot with a shotgun, it was people food and garbage that sealed his fate. When visiting the Park, put all your garbage and food scraps of every kind inside the bear-proof dumpsters and make sure the lid latches. Or take your trash out with you when you leave.

A fed bear is a dead bear. Remember when you're in the Park, it's their home. We are only visitors.

APPENDIX 1

ENCOUNTERING BLACK BEARS IN THE SMOKIES

Bears are a lot like people. Each one has a different personality, and every day brings new situations which affect their mood. Bears will act differently when they're hungry, scared, or upset, in the same way people will be more short-tempered if they're on a diet or if they're being harassed while they're trying to eat.

Bear behavior is sometimes unpredictable. We can observe them and learn a lot, but we'll never be able to predict in advance what a particular animal will do in every situation.

The Great Smoky Mountains National Park attracts over nine million people a year who come to enjoy the views and learn about the flora, fauna, history, and culture of the region. The Park is one of the few remaining places of refuge for wild black bears, *Ursus americanus*, and the Park's bears are its most popular residents.

Please keep in mind when you're viewing bears that we're compromising their world. So, we need to go the extra mile not to interfere with them or endanger them.

Here are a few key points you should keep in mind when encountering a black bear. Be very careful how you manage the food you bring into the Park and the scraps and garbage you leave behind. Food that isn't secured and scraps or garbage that isn't properly disposed of cause the biggest problems in keeping bears and tourists safe and healthy.

This is how it happens—a wild bear cub is taught by its mother to stay away from people, to be afraid of them, but when they smell food in a picnic area at night and don't see any people around, they might take a chance and wander in to look for food scraps.

When a bear gets food this way, it's encouraged to take bigger and bigger chances. It'll get bolder and will start to forage in the daytime and eventually things will escalate to the point that the bear is foraging in the daytime when people are around.

As you've read in the stories in this book, a bear that has lost its fear of people usually results in problems. So, when this happens, rangers try to stop the positive rewards (food and garbage) and reverse the process, if possible.

Training bears to stay away from human food is easier if they're caught in their earliest misbehaviors. A bear that starts to regularly visit a picnic area or campground at night is caught in a live capture culvert trap. Then it is immobilized with drugs, ear tagged, and tattooed for identification purposes, and has a small non-functional tooth pulled to determine how old they are. The bear is then released as close as possible to where it was caught.

If the unpleasant, negative memory of being captured and dominated by a human is stronger than the positive experience of getting food or scraps, the bear will usually re-develop a fear of people and won't come back to the area, at least not when people are present.

Although the experience for the bear during a temporary capture may be unpleasant, it helps to protect the bear from us. Humans are the only black bear predator. If they're safe from us, they live longer lives.

The Great Smoky Mountain National Park covers 800 square miles, and we have approximately 1,600 bears in the Park, so that's about two bears per square mile. That's a lot of bears using the same area as our nine million tourists. This is why it's important for visitors to understand a few basic principles. If you're wondering how you should behave when you come into an area with a bear, here are some brief guidelines.

Don't get so close to the bear that you disturb its natural feeding behavior. Park regulations forbid people from intentionally approaching closer than fifty yards, or any other distance that would disturb or displace the animal.

If a bear approaches you when you're outside the Park, at a cabin for example, try to quickly secure any food you have outside, get it inside the cabin or into a vehicle, then retreat to the inside of the cabin or vehicle. Don't run away from the animal. Don't leave any garbage whatsoever out at night, not even birdseed in a feeder or a fruit rind tossed into the bushes. It's potentially the most harmful thing you can do.

If a bear approaches you when you are inside the Park, don't turn and run. Don't climb a tree. This might provoke a chase response, and bears are excellent at running and climbing trees. Walk away slowly. Talk to the bear in a soft voice while you are walking away, so it can tell you are leaving.

If a bear approaches you when you are in a campground, look around and see what food you have available. Try to quickly secure it inside a camper or vehicle. If you need to, try to scare the bear away. Make noise and throw things at the bear. Then report the incident to the rangers.

If a bear approaches you when you are on a hiking trail, it's important to determine the reason it's coming toward you, so you can make the appropriate response. If you encounter a bear and it swats the ground with its paws and makes huffing noises, this usually indicates a defensive behavior. The bear is telling you that you are too close. So what should you do?

You should slowly back up and give the bear some space, talking in a calm tone. If a bear persists in approaching you without vocalizing or swatting its paws, the reason for its approach is not always clear. It's possible the bear is trying to determine what you are, or it may be after your food; or, in rare cases, it may consider you as prey. This is serious.

If this happens, talk to the bear in a low tone and slowly back up. If the bear continues toward you, change your direction. If the bear is getting closer, gather your group together and stand your ground. Start talking in a very loud and authoritative voice. Make yourself and your group look as big possible. Stand on a log or rock and throw sticks and rocks as you yell. Act dominant, authoritative, and forceful.

Make as much noise as you can, but stand your ground. Do not run. You cannot outrun or outclimb a bear. You need to quickly establish dominance over the approaching bear.

If you think the bear is after your food—if, for example, it runs over to investigate what you've thrown at it—that usually indicates that someone has thrown food to the bear in the past and that's what it wants. If it continues toward you and makes contact with you—grabs, slaps, or bites you—quickly separate yourself from your food.

Take your backpack off and back away slowly, talking to the animal as you back up. If you don't think the bear is after your food and you're physically attacked, fight back with anything possible. Playing dead is not a good strategy when dealing with black bears in the Smokies.

When you know and do the right things, you not only help protect yourself, but also you protect the other visitors and the bears in the Great Smoky Mountains National Park.

APPENDIX 2

THINGS I LEARNED DURING MY CAREER WITH THE NATIONAL PARK SERVICE

- Large wild animals are easier to manage than people.

- When managing animals, experience is the best teacher.

- Bears and wild hogs smell really, really bad.

- During my career, the bear population increased fourfold, from 400 to 1,600.

- During my career, my weight increased by forty pounds.

- When trapping black bears, fresh Krispy Kreme doughnuts are the secret weapon for bait. They worked on me too.

- Eating a Whopper at Burger King seemed, at the time, to relieve stress.

- Hiking up and down the Smoky Mountains eating freeze dried food, beanee weenee, and ramen noodles caused me to lose weight.

- A pig is a pig is a pig! Wild hogs eat enormous amounts of food that is critical to the survival of bears and other wildlife in the mountains.

- Bears never weigh as much as visitors think they weigh.

- When hiring summer wildlife field staff, I'd always ask if they could carry a forty pound pack and hike ten miles through rough mountainous terrain. Every applicant said *yes*, but they weren't

BEAR IN THE BACK SEAT

always telling the truth!

- I used to think I'd always be able to carry a sixty pound pack to the top of the Smokies. I was wrong!

- I used to think that because I was a government employee, the police wouldn't give me a speeding ticket. I was wrong!

- I thought when I retired I'd have a million dollars in the bank to live on. I was wrong again.

- I thought when I graduated from college, I'd never ever have to write a letter, give a presentation, or use a computer again. I was wrong!

- When I began my NPS career, I had no cell phone, GPS, text messaging, Twitter, Facebook, or laptop computer.

- New critters that showed up during my years in the Park were peregrine falcons, river otters, barn owls, coyotes, red wolves, and elk.

- I've learned that sometimes it's the small things in life that matter. I learned this after accidentally drinking some contaminated water on the trail.

- Many people are willing to work for less money in a job that makes them happy.

- Working in the field is much less stressful than working at Park Headquarters.

- Are people smarter than the average bear? I have seen several situations that clearly demonstrate this is not the case.

- Wild animals in the mountains are much smarter than we give them credit for.

- Most visitors to the Park are intelligent people but, for some reason, when they see a wild animal like a bear, hog, or an elk, many of them go temporarily insane and run after the animals to try to feed, or touch, or photograph them.

- Too many people in this world are raised on concrete and asphalt and are very naïve about nature and wild animal behavior.

- I was always humbled by the gratitude and appreciation that people expressed to rangers for caring for wildlife in the mountains.

- If I had the chance to start over and pick any career in life, I'd feel fortunate and blessed if I could do the exact same thing over again.

You can get in touch with Kim by email at BlackBearBook@gmail.com

His Facebook page is https://www.facebook.com/BlackBearBook

His Twitter address is https://twitter.com/BlackBearBook

Kim is an experienced speaker, teacher, and workshop leader. Contact him at BlackBearBook@gmail.com if you'd like to schedule an event.

If you'd like Kim to autograph you book, mail it, along with return postage, to:

E. Kim DeLozier

229 South Shiloh Road

Seymour, TN 37865

DEDICATION

Kim DeLozier

This book is dedicated first and foremost to my Lord and Savior, Jesus Christ, who provides my strength and guidance each and every day. I am so thankful to Him just to be born in America where at least I live in a free country and for being raised by two outstanding Christian parents, Bill and Barbara. Over thirty years ago, God also graciously blessed my life with a wonderful wife and two healthy children, and to top it off, He gave me a career that was tailor made just for me. For that, I am eternally grateful.

Without hesitation, my next line of support in my life comes from my wife and best friend, Donna. She has always been there to keep me on the straight and narrow. She was there to help me when I didn't really deserve to be helped, and love me when I didn't deserve to be loved, and listened to me when she really did not want to listen. She successfully held down the fort for our family on countless nights that I was away either camping in the backcountry or gone for an out of town meeting or event. Although, she occasionally said she was scared at night, she never really seriously complained. She always asked, "Honey, when will you be home?" Donna was also the primary leader in raising our two children and raised them far better than I could have ever done alone. She was also able to keep them in order by saying, "You do that again and I promise you that I'll tell your Dad when he comes home." I appreciate her willingness and professionalism in answering the hundreds of phone calls relating to my job in managing the critters in the Park. I can still hear her now giving advice to a fearful caller that had just seen a bear, "Sir, just be sure to put your garbage inside and do not leave any dog or cat food outside. Everything will be okay then." Without Donna's support, concern, and love for me, I would not have had success in handling the demanding and sometimes stressful times in my job and for that, I am forever indebted and extremely grateful to her.

Mom died on October 23, 2007 but I feel she is still beside me every day. I especially want to dedicate this book to her for her unconditional love, never ending support and her sincere encouragement. Because she was always there to help me along, I was the first in our family to graduate from college. She knew I did not like school. She always told me that I could do whatever I set my mind to do. I believed her. Along with Mom's support and encouragement was that from my Dad, Bill. We spent many days together cutting tobacco, feeding chickens, chasing cows (or them chasing us), hauling hay, or fixing a fence. I appreciate him for giving me the opportunity to grow up and work on the family farm. The values he instilled in me will stay with me forever. His conservative financial guidance and mentoring is still alive and well in me today; just ask my family. Mom and Dad, thanks for all you did in providing me a life that anyone would be proud of and fortunate to have.

I also dedicate this book to my children, Carrie and Travis, and their wonderful families. I appreciate them for the life decisions they have made and continue to make as they grow older. They lived through the years when I was gone because of work related things. Travis is just a chip off the ole block, but a much better one. I do want to say that I'm sorry to him for scarring him for life by intentionally scaring him when around a bear, wild hog, or snake. Maybe he will get over it, but I doubt it. Travis is a great Dad to his two boys and a person I feel fortunate to call my son. I appreciate Carrie for being a great mother to her two boys and for being such a good friend to so many. I could not ask for a better daughter. I'm also thankful for her letting me win a few friendly arguments between us. She was always better. Seriously, I am so proud of my kids and their families. I love them, appreciate them and am very, very proud to call them my family. They are surely one of my biggest blessings in life.

Finally, I'd like to dedicate this book to all those co-workers, supervisors, and employees that gave of themselves to ensure that wild animals in the Smokies have a home forever. All the many calls after hours, the late work schedules, working on weekends and holidays, the call-ins are all reminders of the kind of top notch professionals I was fortunate to work with. The constant dedication, concern, and devotion shown are why wildlife in the Park is well today. Although the list of all the people that supported and helped me is too long to mention, I do want to give a special thanks to Bill Stiver, Carroll Schell, Joe Abrell, Stu Coleman, Bill Cook, Buck Branham, Rick Varner, Chuck Hester, Blake McCann, Jay Clark, Jennifer Murrow, Dale Raxter, Terry Esker, Bob Koerkenmeier, and Dan Nolfi. Also, kudos goes out to Dr. John New and Dr. Ed Ramsay from the University of Tennessee for their guidance, knowledge, and veterinarian expertise in caring for the health of our critters. Also, thanks to all those from Appalachian Bear Rescue for giving many unfortunate bears a second chance to return to the wild.

I owe my life, career, and accomplishments to so many. I pray God would graciously bless them every day of their lives. If wild animals in the Smoky Mountains could talk, I know they would thank them too.

Carolyn Jourdan

This book is dedicated with deep respect, admiration, and affection to the wildlife rangers in the Great Smoky Mountains National Park.

Although they wear their heroism with great modesty, these rangers risk their lives on a routine basis to protect the more than nine million people who visit the Great Smoky Mountains National Park every year, as well as each other, and the bears, elk, and other wildlife in the Park.

Made in the USA
San Bernardino, CA
19 March 2014